PRAISE FOR GEORGIA FOSTER'S DRINK LESS PROGRAMME

'Georgia specialises in alcohol hypnosis. Her task is to show us how to repro-
gramme our subconscious mind (which has an effect on bodil⌐ ⌐nctions such
as the heart, lungs and digestion) to need less alcohol... ᵀ ᵢlliant day
– and it worked... My skin was clearer and I slept be⌐ ˦ of the
week, my usual total of 40 units is down to a mor⌐ ˋanks
to hypnotherapy... And the brilliant thing? ᴵ ˙ng
alcohol completely.'

Daily Mail

'[Georgia] doesn't forbid alcohol but s⌐ ⌐ need less. I appreciate
not feeling destroyed next day...The bri⌐ ₒ⌐ I haven't had to give up
completely. But I've learned one crucial poi⌐ ⌐s not how much you drink, it's
why you drink.'

Evening Standard

'I don't know if it's because I have more energy and am more active, but I've
lost half a stone. People keep saying how well I look. Yesterday, someone asked
me if I'd had a facelift. I thought I needed alcohol to relax, to make life more
interesting, to make me more interesting. It's not true.'

Independent

'Clinical Hypnotherapist, Georgia Foster, says about a third of her clients – mostly
professionals and financial types – have alcohol related problems. "Drinking in the
city is like a sport, although the consequences are swept under the carpet... It's all
too easy to get into this sort of situation – it can happen to any of us – and unless you
get help or sort it out, it can easily wreck your life."'

The Sunday Times

'For everyone with what Georgia calls "an over-drinking problem," she has
synthesised her treatment approach into a practical, easy-to follow book...'

You magazine

'With a programme to stick to, it's not as hard as I imagined... I still have cravings
for alcohol, but have just had five small glasses of wine in the past 10 days – a huge
improvement... I feel stronger and more accepting of my current situation, so
there was less of an internal struggle and less of a void to fill with drink.'

Psychologies magazine

DRINK LESS IN 7 DAYS

GEORGIA FOSTER

RedDoor

Published by RedDoor
www.reddoorpublishing.com

ISBN 978-1-910453-57-5

A CIP catalogue record for this book is available from the British Library
Add near the credits at the bottom:

Music composed by Christopher Lloyd Clarke
https://enlightenedaudio.com

Recordings engineered by Jimi Lloyd-Wyatt
Producer/Mixer/Engineer
www.ginger-studios.com

Cover design and typesetting: Megan Sheer
Print managed by Jellyfish Solutions Ltd

CONTENTS

INTRODUCTION

- Are you worried about how much you drink but just can't cut back?

- Do family and friends criticise your drinking?

- Do you love a drink or two, but want to drink less?

- Does feeling guilty and anxious about your drinking make you drink more?

The good news is, there is nothing wrong with you!

I have written this book specifically to help people who are secretly worried about how much alcohol they drink, so that they can learn how to drink less without having to rely on willpower!

I don't know how many times drinking clients tell me they dread going to the doctor knowing they may be asked: 'How many units or standard glasses do you drink a week?' They shrink with fear, knowing the little white lie will need to come out to protect them. 'Eh, ummm ... just a few glasses a night, a few days a week.' The drinker often feels anxious that they will be chastised like a child or made to feel guilty that they don't have a better handle on their drinking life.

There may be some family members, friends or, even worse, a child who suggests that you should be drinking less. Of course, this is suggested with the best intentions and comes from a place of care and love. My question is: 'Does it stop the drinking or reduce it?' In my experience, rarely! In fact, the opposite can take place, where over-consumption increases because of the fear that there really is a drinking issue to worry about.

WHY WRITE THIS BOOK?

I'm a clinical hypnotherapist and I've been in the business of helping people to drink less since 1994. Since qualifying with distinction with The London College of Clinical Hypnosis, I have tirelessly spent years learning about how drinkers think and feel. I can assure my absolute support in helping you to drink less with my special approach. If we all went to our doctor and took their advice on adopting a healthy level of alcohol consumption, that would be the end of the problem. If it was that easy to just cut back, everyone would drink within the healthy range and I wouldn't have written this book.

I am constantly frustrated by how often people are judged and criticised for how much alcohol they drink, because this can send them underground with their drinking. They may start to 'sneaky drink' because they become self-conscious that people think they drink too much. The vicious cycle continues and ultimately the drinking issue becomes a bigger problem than it originally was.

WHO IS THIS BOOK FOR?

When I run one of my Drink Less Mind seminars, people who attend tell me that they are pleasantly surprised and equally relieved to find themselves sitting next to a doctor, lawyer, accountant, homemaker, retiree or an entrepreneur. These people, just like you, are hard-working and good citizens in society, who just happen to drink more than they truly want to.

These people don't want to abstain but equally, just can't seem to cut back. They seek out my approach because they want to learn how to achieve the middle ground of drinking. The subject of drinking too much is taboo, and the person who truly wants to drink less can be made to feel like an alcoholic who will have to quit drinking altogether.

The other day, a client said she was horrified that her 14-year-old daughter had started to count how many glasses of wine she was drinking. Sarah knew she was drinking too much but thought it was going under the radar of her child. I asked Sarah, did you start drinking less knowing your daughter was watching you?' Embarrassed, Sarah admitted, 'No. In fact I was drinking more.' She couldn't understand why her drinking was increasing and yet she knew how much this was worrying her daughter.

Sarah then went on to explain this awful feeling that her daughter was micro-managing her drinking. This led her to have a secret wine stash, so her daughter thought she was drinking from one bottle when it was actually two.

Sarah is very typical of the millions of over-drinking people living on this planet. Like her, they know they drink too much but just don't know how to cut back. But they know they don't belong in Alcoholics Anonymous either.

Whether you are a mum who likes to unwind at the end of the day with a few glasses too many or the business traveller who gets bored and drinks as a form of entertainment, I want you to know that you are far from alone. The truth is, nobody likes a hangover and waking up feeling awful about what they drank the night before.

Many people drink because they are socially shy, lonely, bored, unhappy, scared, want to numb difficult feelings or are worried about their future. For others, alcohol can offer them salvation from living in a stressful situation or an aid to sleeping. There are many reasons why people drink too much.

I know many people who scorn laughter and frivolity when they are sober, but after a few drinks they begin to laugh and enjoy themselves.

Many people have trained themselves emotionally, through the software of their mind, that drinking is a laughter pill and without it, life is just plain hard.

As a therapist, author and speaker on this important subject, I find websites that focus on alcohol consumption generally unhelpful. Often they ask you to tick the box if you think about drinking before 9 a.m. in the morning. Or if you say yes to drinking alcohol on your own, you have a problem. Or even worse, 'If you lie about your drinking you need to go to Alcoholics Anonymous'!

I respect that there needs to be guidelines and responsible information is important as a resourceful tool. However, it can often feel heavy-handed with a sprinkle of scaremongering, which can exacerbate the drinking problem. Throw in a couple of articles in the media about the connection to alcohol-related cancer, liver issues, brain cells dying and more, and it's enough to drive you to drink!

The truth is, it does appear to be difficult to drink less. Often people abstain for months or even years because they just can't seem to drink regularly in a balanced way, because they don't trust themselves.

I can assure you, there is another way. I believe my approach will enable you to move on from unhelpful ways of thinking about drinking days. My goal is to liberate you from the over-drinking treadmill, so you can have a healthier and happier relationship with alcohol. You can start to enjoy what you drink guilt-free, while regularly drinking less. This book can help you to learn to drink less, easily and effectively, irrespective of your past. This book is not for alcoholics but for people who have got themselves into a bit of a bad drinking habit that is causing them some grief.

However, if you have experienced sexual, physical or emotional abuse, or feel you have unresolved psychological issues, alcohol could lead to dependency, recreational drugs or worse. *If you feel this is your situation, please seek out a reputable therapist.*

I want you to live your life without feeling the shame and embarrassment of the over-drinking habit. I want you to embrace your life in ways that enhance it, rather than restrict it, because of your drinking.

> *There is nothing wrong with you! I believe it's your thinking, not your drinking, that is the real problem.*

In other words, the thinking process that occurs before that gin and tonic, beer or wine even touches your lips is the problem. I can assure you it is a habit. A habit that can be unlearned. The tools I will give you will help you to drink less, irrespective of how much you were drinking before or for how long.

So if you are tired of feeling guilty about being single and living on your own while enjoying wine with your meal and your favourite show, stop now!

If you sneaky drink to stop family members from giving you the evil eye, keep reading!

If life just is too stressful and you need to drink alcohol as a way to shut out difficult feelings, this book will help you understand this cycle of negative thinking and how to move out of it.

If you use the tools and techniques in this book, you will not only learn how to drink less but create new, healthier coping strategies without the drinking too much crutch. You will learn profound techniques that will release you from the years of fear and angst about your relationship with alcohol. Specifically, you will learn a powerful psychological approach that has helped people all over the world to realise their true potential.

The strong strategy that I outline will help you to drink less over seven days and beyond.

It's time for you to manage your alcohol consumption, rather than let it manage you.

There are two twenty-five-minute Hypnosis Hub recordings and two five-minute Hypno Blast recordings included with this book. If you suffer from epilepsy or have any concerns, please consult your doctor before listening to the recordings. All you have to do is to sign up with your name and email address to access these recordings at: www.georgiafoster.com/hypnosishub.

CHAPTER 1

THE SOFTWARE OF YOUR MIND

What I love about the special work I do to help people drink less is the science behind it.

Many years ago when I first became a specialist in alcohol reduction, my approach was seen as being a bit out there. I struggled to get it accepted. I am pleased to inform you that my methods are now backed up by many neuro-scientists around the world.

I believe that your drinking, irrespective of your personal history, is a habit. A habit that you can unlearn.

I respect that there are people out there who have had alcoholic tendencies and may be alcoholics. There are people who have been labelled as alcoholics and believe this to be true. I am not here to advise you who fits the alcoholic criteria, although, I might add, there are many clients who thought they did, and were relieved to know that they were not alcoholics.

This book is not for alcoholics. This book is for people who know they need to drink less but just don't know how.

Sounds too simple?

The way the brain functions is the problem when it comes to drinking too much in unhealthy ways. I can confidently say I know that this part of the mind is very good at maintaining a drinking problem. It's not because your brain wants to be unhelpful but rather the opposite. It thinks it is being really helpful when it comes to your drinking behaviour.

Why?

Your brain has learned to think how you drink is normal. It doesn't make your drinking right or wrong; the mind just takes what is familiar to be correct.

THERE IS NO SUCH THING AS WILLPOWER

The mind is a powerful tool and can appear to work against your best-laid plans. In my opinion, willpower doesn't exist. It's just a way to keep you on the hamster wheel of regular frustration as to why you can't seem to get out of this unhelpful drinking cycle.

THE AMYGDALA

We have two choices when it comes to how we respond to life. They are positive and negative. These responses have a direct correlation to what emotions we are feeling at any given time.

What neuroscientists have known for some time is that when someone feels scared a particular part of the brain called the amygdala lights up. The amygdala is made up of two almond-shaped nerve tissues located on either side of the brain. This is responsible for emotions; in particular, fear and being in survival mode. Equally, it is the part of the brain that deals with the perception of anger, sadness and aggression. One of its most important roles is to verify these emotions in similar situations that may arise in the future.

A great example of how the amygdala works in relationship to alcohol is to think about when you have felt scared, lonely or unsafe and you have instantly thought of drinking alcohol.

It could be that you have an important meeting or have to deal with a personal situation that causes you to feel stressed. In a nanosecond your brain will go to the amygdala, which sends a distress signal to the hypothalamus triggering stress chemicals such as cortisol and adrenaline. Your brain and body don't like this feeling. Here, your mind has to make a decision to stay stressed and deal with it or find a quick solution to move you out of this scary space. This is often called the fight or flight syndrome.

If it is the appropriate time for you to drink, you may choose to drink. Flying away with alcohol works so well because it instantly shuts down the amygdala and the brain says 'thank you' for calming you down. What is interesting is this feeling of being unsafe works on memory.

There are many drinkers out there who feel ashamed and full of guilt about their relationship with alcohol. They don't understand why they just can't drink less. However, I can assure you if your brain has trained itself to use alcohol to shut down the amygdala, it will be very difficult to change this mechanism with willpower alone. This is because turning to alcohol in order to feel better quickly has become habit or, to put it another way, a brilliant protective mechanism that takes you away from the amygdala. Your brain thinks it is working really well to keep you feeling safe. So if you are feeling trapped and frustrated, as well as angry at yourself about your drinking, remember the amygdala! I can assure you that you are not a hopeless case.

When you feel bad you are instantly firing off the amygdala and then, without even thinking, you have triggered the desire to drink when you know you don't want to.

Alcohol shuts down the amygdala very quickly, so it is no surprise that the first alcoholic drink you consume is fast and furious, because your brain is demanding you calm yourself down now!

The first glass is often medicinal. The demand from the amygdala is so unconscious that you may not even be aware of it. So, as much as you may try to change this behaviour (which is why this book is so important), consciously it will be difficult to do.

The trigger doesn't have to be a big, stressful situation; it could simply be that you are bored or tired and alcohol gives you some energy. It could be that you are feeling socially shy and need a quick drink to calm your anxiety down. There are many reasons why we drink when we don't want to. I want to help you change this chicken and egg problem.

My drink less in seven days approach gives you an opportunity to create a new, healthier communication with a different part of the brain.

Like yin and yang, like night and day, even the most guilt-ridden and anxious drinker has the potential to trigger a thinking process that embodies calm and logic without the use of alcohol.

The brain and body cannot live life permanently with the amygdala running the show. Of course, for someone who has extreme high levels of anxiety, this can be true. Even so, the brain and body can at some stage learn how to extinguish this uncomfortable response.

THE PREFRONTAL CORTEX

The prefrontal cortex is the executive decision-maker of the brain and works in conjunction with the amygdala. When the amygdala triggers a perceived threat, the prefrontal cortex will decide how this should be handled. Generally, the prefrontal cortex regulates decisions, but if someone is exposed to high levels of anxiety or regular bouts of fear, an imbalance in logical thinking can occur.

This is when alcohol becomes a player in calming the brain and body down.

As soon as alcohol is consumed, it starts to affect the brain chemistry by affecting our neurotransmitters. These are the chemical messengers that transmit signals throughout the body.

Alcohol affects both excitatory and inhibitory neurotransmitters. Glutamate, the excitatory neurotransmitter, normally increases brain activity and energy levels, but alcohol has the opposite effect of slowing down this transmitter. GABA, the inhibitory neurotransmitter that is normally responsible for calming you down and reducing energy, is increased by alcohol intake. Alcohol stimulates the GABA brain receptors, very much like the effect of taking drugs such as Valium and other tranquillizers, resulting in a feeling of being relaxed. As GABA increases we start to chill out more and don't care so much about the stresses and strains of life. The increase in GABA means speech and physical movements slow down, hence the staggering around and falling over that can occur as alcohol consumption continues.

What also increases when you drink alcohol is dopamine, the chemical that is located in the 'reward' area of your brain. If alcohol is something you use to dampen the stresses and strains of life, dopamine is a great way to escape. After a period of time your brain gets used to it and welcomes the extra dopamine and the GABA transmitters too. Before you know it, the brain demands this chemical reaction when you have any stirrings of feeling vulnerable. Your brain becomes familiar with this brain transaction, which is when the habit of drinking to deal with life starts to cement itself.

Over a period of time the sensations that dopamine creates diminishes, which is why people then need more alcohol to experience the same feeling. The alcohol consumption goes up as the tolerance to more alcohol becomes noted by the brain.

The goal of this book, in conjunction with the Hypnosis Hub recordings, is to keep your brain focused in the prefrontal cortex before you drink and when you drink. The longer you stay in the prefrontal cortex part of your brain, the more in control you are of your drinking in positive ways. It remains the master of your logical ship, steering you away from unhelpful over-drinking.

When someone feels safe, logical and trusting in their drinking relationship they drink slowly because the prefrontal cortex remains at the helm. Their mind doesn't demand the GABA and dopamine hit because they have learned another way to produce those chemicals during the day before they have their first drink.

THE THIRD EYE

For those who lead a spiritual life, you may be familiar with the concept of the third eye. For centuries sages have suggested this part of our minds as the key to feeling more centred, calm and grounded. It is exactly where the prefrontal cortex is located.

In the past, there have been many people who brushed this off as mumbo jumbo; however, it has now been confirmed that this area of the brain is exactly where we are when we are intuitive and make rational decisions.

Keeping the prefrontal cortex present is key when it comes to how you react to your life. Without it, high levels of anxiety can occur, which can lead to alcohol dependency.

The prefrontal cortex is instrumental in keeping you in a safe place and this is why the Hypnosis Hub recordings are so important. It is fully available to anyone, including you as a drinker! Can you imagine a life where your brain and body are more present in the prefrontal cortex rather than the amygdala?

Your drinking history is a habit *you can change*.

Your brain and body need to develop new coping strategies that reflect not being so emotionally present in the space of the amygdala, but rather in balance with the prefrontal cortex, so that this part of the brain can regulate reality versus unhelpful thinking.

Yes, it does take practice, but the recordings will help your mind and body learn healthier coping strategies that go straight to the prefrontal cortex rather than to your favourite alcoholic tipple.

The aim is to get your brain and body in a good space before your first sip of alcohol. Then you won't have this urgency to drink to calm yourself down. Your whole entire sense of self-worth will increase. Your mind will know that alcohol is something to enjoy rather than to gulp in the mad moments of stress, anger or whatever you are feeling. We know how you respond to your life is key. If someone is nervous and fearful about life (glass half-empty) they will often catastrophise the situation, playing out unhelpful scenes in their minds, which is driven by the amygdala. Whereas someone who is in the prefrontal cortex sees the situation as something to be dealt with as best as can be and can distinguish the truth from the drama (glass half-full).

One of the goals of this book is to retrain your mind and body to be more present in your daily life, with the prefrontal cortex running the show. That way you will experience a sense of emotional wellbeing even through challenging times.

This means your amygdala won't be firing off so much and the pressure to drink quickly and as often won't be there.

UNCONSCIOUS DRINKING

I am not suggesting if you win the lottery tonight that you shouldn't drink a little bit too much champagne. That is a different sort of drinking. That is called fun and happy drinking. What I am talking about is the regular, habitual drinking that stops you from feeling good about you.

It's your regular automated drinking that horrifies you when you realise half a bottle of wine has been consumed while you are chopping the vegetables. Or that fourth bottle of beer seems to have gone down rather quickly as you mow the lawn or while you are doing your accounting at the end of the day.

FELICITY'S DRINKING STORY

Felicity finally realised how much she was drinking but just couldn't get herself out of the habit. Her drinking wasn't necessarily related to high levels of stress but rather it had become a way of life that was getting a little out of control.

Her day was demanding but she thrived on it too, and her way to stop her 'busy brain' was to come home and cook. Her ritual was to come in the door, get the kids' meals ready, while having one large glass of wine. She would then get her kids ready for bed, while another glass hovered. By the time she and her husband came home, she was back in the kitchen preparing a meal for the two of them with another glass of wine.

By this stage it was 8.15 p.m. and almost a whole bottle of wine had been consumed. Felicity knew it was too much and felt guilty that by the time her and her husband sat down she was ready to open another bottle.

I hear this kind of story so often. People are bored and tired of this sort of habitual drinking but just can't seem to stop doing it.

Felicity wasn't necessarily stressed but her demanding job keeps her adrenaline going, which means her amygdala was still firing off to a certain level into the evening. Felicity didn't know that her brain was demanding she drink as a way to relax her.

Felicity started listening to one of my recordings about training her mind and body to be calmer before she walked in the door. Just this one technique adjusted her drinking from nearly two bottles of wine a night to just under one. Her habitual drinking changed to a healthier habit of alternating one wine for one big glass of water, and this then became her normal evening ritual.

It's the ritualistic drinking that is so often the problem, which is why it can go unnoticed for such a long time. This is because it is classed as not being problem drinking.

People become acclimatised to a certain amount of alcohol. As explained before the tolerance goes up, a bit like when someone's appetite increases, because the brain gets used to the dopamine. So it's no surprise that one glass of alcohol over a period of time doesn't do the job and more alcohol needs to be consumed to relax and unwind.

EMOTIONAL CONDITIONING

Many people seek my help because, unlike Felicity, they are going through a very traumatic time and are using alcohol as their emotional crutch.

They may not normally be a big drinker but higher levels of stress and life's challenges drive them to drink. This is because the amygdala scans their history and the history of others who have been through trauma to locate a quick solution to bring some sort of homeostasis to the situation. If that person's mind brings up alcohol, it will demand it for some respite.

TOM'S STORY

Tom wife's had been diagnosed with terminal breast cancer. He had a daily ritual of saying goodnight to his wife, then sitting down with some stiff whiskys. He said it was his time to be just by himself and what I call having a 'solo party'. Tom had not been a big drinker before her diagnosis. He said he had the occasional hangover but since his wife had been ill he was drinking a lot of whisky, mainly on his own after his wife had gone to bed.

I think we would all agree that Tom's drinking was utterly understandable; there is nothing wrong with drinking on your own and this time was important to him after a busy day looking after his wife's needs. And yet, Tom felt his drinking was affecting the precious time he had left with his wife, as he was often under par when she woke in the morning.

By the time Tom came to see me he was emotionally exhausted. I often ask this question of my clients: 'Who looks after you?' They look stunned. Then I ask them again, 'Who really looks after you?' Usually the answer is 'no one' and in Tom's case, this was also true.

He was a beaten man, faced with the truth that he was going to lose his precious wife, which is why he felt so guilty about his drinking. He said to me, 'Georgia, I get so angry with myself that I sit up night after night on my own drinking. I know full well when I wake in the morning my quality of time with my wife is important. So why would I want to sabotage it by drinking too much and waking feeling awful? Logically I know I don't need those two extra whiskies and yet I keep doing it night after night.'

My heart goes out to anybody who is in a similar situation because, from my perspective, Tom needs his own space. However, it was getting a little out of hand.

Tom agreed that he would listen to one of my recordings that helps people to take time out of their emotionally demanding life and just be in the moment.

This recording was instrumental in Tom's time out from the amygdala. While he listened he was helping his mind and body have time in the prefrontal cortex rather than relying on alcohol to achieve this quiet zone. Over a period of two weeks he started to notice that he didn't need those two extra whiskies. His mind now knew there was another way to find some space without a glass in his hand.

BECOMING FAMILIAR

When your brain and body become familiar with this lovely, healthy habit of drinking less, you will be able to enjoy the freedom of drinking without the angst and the guilt.

Becoming familiar is key here because habits need to be learned and it does take practice; hence why the recordings are so important.

After chapter 2, you will be ready to start listening to the first twenty-five minute Hypnosis Hub recording called Track 1, which is really exciting, as this is where the powerful brain training will occur.

Using hypnosis to drink less alcohol

Some people are nervous when I mention I am a clinical hypnotherapist because of the stories they have heard about stage hypnosis. I can reassure you that hypnosis is one of the most effective methods to reduce alcohol consumption. If I had a pound or dollar for every time someone said to me 'I couldn't possibly be hypnotised' I would have enough for an extra-special beach holiday every year!

Everybody, including you and me, can be hypnotised, which is good news because your mind is an incredible tool when utilised properly. Hypnosis is, to my knowledge, one of, if not the quickest and most effective methods, to learn how to drink less. It is a brilliant way to shift your brain and body to a safer place where you will feel calm and logical about your life, so you can decide to drink without the fear and self-doubt of drinking too much.

Hypnosis is a natural brainwave phenomenon that occurs when we daydream and don't remember exactly what happened; for example, how we drove from A to B or we are sitting on a train and suddenly we are at our destination.

While in the daydream state your conscious mind drifts away while your unconscious mind is wide awake (and is always awake even while you go to sleep). During this time you are in a heightened state of suggestion whether in an alert state of hypnosis or in the sleep state. Either works really well. The analytical part of the brain shuts down and the problem-solving area of the brain is heightened. That is not to suggest that you can resolve all problems while in hypnosis but rather, while in this state, amazing emotional intelligence can occur. The statement 'Sleep on it, the answer will come in the morning' is actually true.

Many people assume the conscious mind is clever; in fact, it is the unconscious mind that does all the heavy lifting. When utilised properly, results are fast!

TIME IS IRRELEVANT

Your unconscious mind doesn't understand the concept of time, hence why you can remember certain things clearly that happened years ago. This is why you can recall when you played hide and seek with a neighbour when you were seven, or a present-day conversation triggers the memory of something funny when you were twelve.

PROGRESSIVE APPROACH

Although I, like most hypnotherapists, am trained in regression therapy, professionally I believe there is a better way.

I call myself a progressive therapist. When I explain this to my seminar attendees I often see relief on their faces.

I am not suggesting psychotherapy or counselling is unhelpful. I believe many different types of therapy can play a key role to help people feel more whole.

In my experience working with drinkers, part of their problem is their mind is working on the history of their unhelpful drinking as a reference. They keep regurgitating their drinking relationship, trying to understand why they got themselves into this unhelpful drinking cycle in the first place. It goes round and round in their head, leaving them baffled and frustrated at their inability to drink less.

While you continue to assess your drinking behaviour as the truth, using old references, your drinking behaviour will be difficult to change. By references, I mean your memories of the way you handle alcohol in various situations. Perhaps you find it difficult not to glug the wine back at parties, because you lack confidence when chatting to strangers. Creating different references for the future is essential. So in order for you to drink less alcohol, you need to create important memories, or references, in your mind that are stronger and more supportive than your current memories of drinking.

THE ALCOHOLIC GENE: SAM'S STORY

Sam told me a very familiar story about his family history. His father was an alcoholic and was abusive to his mother. His father died some years before we met after a long battle with lung cancer. A prominent doctor once told Sam that he had the 'alcoholic gene' and that he should be very wary of his relationship with alcohol.

Sam didn't realise that this one statement from a respected doctor was firing off fear and anxiety about his potential to become an alcoholic. The memory of his father was firing off the amygdala too. Even though he didn't want to turn into his father, because he was so worried he would, it started to appear to become the truth. This scared him even more as his drinking started to increase.

Sam couldn't understand why he would want to ruin his family life by over-consuming alcohol and why the vicious drinking cycle continued. Sam was very good at alcohol-free days but when he did drink, he blitzed it. His wife was becoming increasingly worried, as he was.

He decided to quit drinking for a few years and then one day it was a friend's wedding where he was catching up with some university friends, he got a little over-excited and he decided he would drink. He doesn't remember much about the evening apart from waking up with his wife furious, refusing to talk to him.

Not long after this incident Sam came to see me to tell me his story.

As I explained to Sam, he didn't have the 'alcoholic gene'. In fact, the opposite was true.

OBSERVATIONAL LEARNING

We can unconsciously mimic our parents' behaviours, some good and some not so good. An example would be the child who becomes phobic about flying because their mother had high levels of anxiety about it. Or the child who suffers from depression because their father did.

Our emotional DNA can change at any time. I believe that when someone like Sam is worried they have inherited alcoholism, it has more to do with their internal beliefs that they have carried from childhood. It could be that Sam overheard his grandmother say, 'alcoholism runs in the family' or 'keep an eye on Sam, just in case he inherits his father's alcohol problem'. It could also be that Sam had experienced high levels of stress and anxiety dealing with his father's alcoholism and family dynamics. There could be so many reasons why Sam drank the way he did, but it didn't mean he was an alcoholic. Sam clearly had a propensity to use alcohol as a way to run away from these fears and the vicious drinking cycle it had led to, but that didn't mean he would ruin his life by drinking.

There are people who are alcoholics and have no family history of alcoholism and there are people who have a family member who has been diagnosed with alcoholism who don't drink at all because they are in fear of becoming one. There is no one size fits all. This book is about helping drinkers to drink less, so if you feel you need some medical advice on this as well as some support, please consult your doctor.

Sam had seen the destruction alcohol had played in his family life, which is why he was in fear of it. In the younger days he knew it was fine to drink too much because it was an acceptable part of growing up. As a 'responsible' adult, he knew his drinking had become a problem.

His unconscious mind used his father's drinking relationship as a reference, even though that was, and still is, detrimental to his emotional wellbeing.

WHAT IS FAMILIAR IS NOT ALWAYS HELPFUL

On some level, Sam's mind was using references that were familiar to him, such as his father drinking too much.

The brain normalises any situation that becomes familiar. Sadly, just as there are people on this planet who weren't born racist, the brain learns to accept a habit as normal. People who smoke don't do it because they want to die early from lung cancer. Until you change this mental connection, the habit will continue.

Sam was relieved that he didn't have to repeat his father's alcoholic habits and instantly his self-esteem improved.

For Sam, it was important to train his mind to move on from old, out of date patterns of thought about alcohol. Equally, it was important for him to recognise that other people's history was not, and never will be, his own.

The personalised recording I made for Sam was training his mind to be who he is rather than anybody else. This really calmed him down because his amygdala stopped firing off the fear of becoming his father. This made him feel safer before he drank alcohol. He stopped living in fear of becoming an alcoholic and started living his life with more trust in his present and future.

THE FOUR BRAINWAVE ACTIVITIES OF THE MIND

There are four different brainwave activities we experience throughout every day and night.

Beta

The beta state is called the waking state, where the conscious mind is going about its daily life, involving rational thinking. It is a logical state. It plans our every movement from eating breakfast through to buying a train ticket when we arrive at the station. The conscious mind is the most prominent part of the mind when we are awake.

Alpha

The alpha state is the half-awake/half-asleep state. It is when you daydream or when you can't remember reading the paper for the past ten minutes. It is a time when your conscious mind is sending the information to the unconscious mind to be absorbed, stored and ready to be recalled later.

During this time we are more intuitive. It can be when you find answers to questions, resolve problems and become highly creative. It is a natural meditative state, which is also a hypnotic state, where emotional changes can take place much more easily.

We all need daydream time, just as children do. In fact, approximately between the ages of seven and twelve, children are predominately in the alpha state. This is the last stage of learning to become more adult, to make logical choices and develop a sense of self.

Theta

Theta is a much deeper state. Some would describe it as the meditative state where you can be in a 'nothingness', a peaceful place. This is the state just before you fall asleep and the brainwave activity just before you wake.

From infancy to around seven years of age, a child will be predominately experiencing this brain frequency. You may think about how much an infant has to learn in its first seven years on this earth: how to walk, talk and make sense of the world it lives in.

The recordings will help you to enter this state where you can learn to drink less and be more present in the prefrontal cortex. While in this space, you are absorbing new ways of learning at a much faster rate.

Delta

Delta is when you are asleep. It is a time when your conscious mind rests. Your unconscious mind is still working away, managing your bodily functions such as breathing and your heart beating. It digests food whilst you are in the sleep mode and gets it ready for you to eliminate.

In order to go to sleep at night and wake in the morning you have to go through the hypnotic state, which is the stage just before you go to sleep and just before you wake in the morning. This is the alpha/theta state. We cannot go to sleep or wake without this important transition. Another example is when you daydream and can't remember going from A to B. The hypnotic state, I believe, is the best way to create healthy changes with minimal effort.

It is a natural state we all enter; in fact, many times a day while going in and out of the daydream state and going in and out of the sleep state.

HYPNOSIS VERSUS MEDITATION

One of the most common questions I get asked is, 'What is the difference between hypnosis and meditation?'

The answer is nothing at all apart from one key difference. While in meditation the goal is to think of nothing and being in a peaceful state. I think meditation is a powerful tool, but for many it is difficult to achieve.

Those who have a busy brain often quit the meditation experience because it seems too hard to achieve this deeper level of nothingness. Whereas with hypnosis, you can be in busy-brain mode as much as you want. The good news is – it doesn't affect the results.

Whether you are drifting deeply or listening to some or all of my words on the recordings, the meaning is being absorbed. So please do not worry if you feel you have focused too much on my words or you have fallen asleep. It is working! Trust me! Just go with it.

THE HYPNOSIS HUB AND HYPNO BLAST RECORDINGS

The link to the Hypnosis Hub recordings takes you to two twenty-five-minute tracks and two shorter five-minute Hypno Blasts. You can start to listen to the first recording at the end of chapter 2. It is important that you are sitting or lying somewhere warm and safe where you will be free to relax. You must be stationary throughout the recordings. If you need to wake at any time, open your eyes. If you suffer from epilepsy or have any concerns, please consult your doctor before listening to the recordings.

Please visit www.georgiafoster.com/hypnosishub.

Q. Will I fall asleep?

A. Some people do fall asleep, and some people stay alert with little moments of mini-sleep states. Either is fine and will not change your results.

Q. When is the best time to listen?

A. The best time is before you go to sleep or when you want to have a little nap. I respect that many people don't want their partner or family members to know they are reading this book. If so, please find a time that is private. Some people like to start their day with the recordings. Whatever works for you, works for me.

Q. What if I don't listen to the recordings for a few days?

A. Try to listen to one of the Hypnosis Hub recordings a few times a week. In busy times, try one of the shorter Hypno Blasts to get you into an instant state of confidence.

DRINK ONE WATER ONE – THE DOWO POLICY

I encourage clients to drink more water on a regular basis. Many clients don't drink enough and mistake the first glass of alcohol as a way to quench their thirst, so it goes down really quickly. Alcohol is a diuretic, therefore it will dehydrate you and will contribute to a hangover the next day.

Start your drinking time with a big glass of water, so your brain and body are hydrated before you start consuming alcohol. Then keep a glass handy with you while you drink. Take a sip of water, then a sip of alcohol, and keep alternating. You will thank yourself in the morning knowing you have hydrated yourself.

During the recordings, I will be helping your mind learn to drink less alcohol and enjoy drinking more water, so enjoy embracing your DOWO policy now!

SOMETHING TO THINK ABOUT

- The fear-based part of your brain thinks drinking is a great way to alleviate you from the amygdala.

- Your mind does know how to tune into the prefrontal cortex with the help of the recordings.

- Your past is your past and it is time to move on and create new, healthier coping strategies without the drive to drink with the same intensity.

CHAPTER 2

THE RADIO-CRAZY SYNDROME

You may not have consciously thought about how you actually talk to yourself. Equally, you may not even be aware of what inner conversations are going on; however, your mind does! Talking to ourselves is natural and sometimes it is positive, but sadly, more often it is not.

How you talk to yourself can be detrimental to the best-laid plans of reducing your drinking. I know so many clients who say to me 'I woke up with such a bad hangover today and I promised myself I wouldn't drink but then the day got on top of me and before I knew it, I was drinking my second beer by 5 p.m.! I am so annoyed with myself. I don't understand why I keep drinking when I know it makes me feel so bad about myself.'

Sounds familiar?

Whatever your inner drinking conversations are about, I can guarantee that most of them, if not all, are hurtful and make you feel bad about your relationship with alcohol.

- Do you wake up in the morning feeling anxious because the first thing you think about is what you said last night after a few drinks?

- Are you surprised, no matter how busy you are, that you can't wait to finish work or get to the end of the day and have *that* drink?

- Do you feel isolated from other people when you don't drink?

- Do certain situations or people trigger you to binge-drink?

- Does drinking help you deal with the stresses and strains of your life?

- Do you feel drinking helps you become more creative and a better problem solver?

- Do you feel anxious eating with people without having a drink?

- Do you love drinking on your own?

- Do you get annoyed when people choose not to drink when you want to?

- Do you drink to communicate?

- Do you drink to feel confident?

- Do you procrastinate about life and put things off by drinking?

- Do you avoid sexual intimacy until you have had a few drinks?

- Do you have drinking buddies who encourage you to over-drink when you don't want to?

- Do you drink to alleviate emotional pain on a regular basis?

If you answered yes to many or all of these questions, this simply demonstrates how much you have tuned into what I call the Radio-crazy Syndrome. This is negative thinking that welcomes excessive and unhelpful drinking. It encourages low self-worth and it supports external judgemental and critical people around you. This syndrome is a drinker's biggest problem.

HOW I DISCOVERED A DIFFERENT PSYCHOLOGICAL APPROACH

In 1994 I went to California and trained with the founders of Voice Dialogue, which is an amazing Jungian psychology. This method profoundly changed my whole approach to my work and the results I was getting with my clients.

In fact, it wasn't just my clients but in my own life too. I used alcohol as a way to deal with my own radio-crazy problem before I found this technique. I can assure you of my utmost confidence that it will help you in more ways than just learning to drink less alcohol!

I've adapted and fine-tuned it over the years, along with some powerful hypnosis techniques that I am offering to you in this book.

MEET YOUR INNER CRITIC

The Voice Dialogue theory is that we are all made up of many parts or sub-personalities. It's like we have little mini-people running around in our heads. Some of these personalities are helpful and others are not.

There is one particular personality I call the Inner Critic. It is the part that is full of doom and gloom about you and your life. It's the part within us all that constantly berates, judges and makes us feel bad, to the point that drives us literally to drink and often too much.

WHAT DOES THE INNER CRITIC SAY ABOUT YOUR DRINKING?

- Do you realise that your work is on the line because of what you said last night, after a few drinks?

- If you hadn't drunk so much at that party, you wouldn't have embarrassed yourself in front of the neighbours.

- You slept with that man/woman last night and you barely know them!

- Women who respect themselves don't drink too much.

- Now you're going to drink and eat all night.

- You'll never lose weight because you can't stop drinking and eating junk food to relax.

- Why can't you just stop at one drink? You have no self-control.

- Your friends secretly think you are an idiot and actually you are!

- Look how much money you spend on alcohol.

- Why do you end up being paranoid or indiscreet when you've had a couple of drinks?

DO YOU HAVE A TALKING MIRROR?

'Your skin looks like crap today – that'll be the wine. Why did you bother getting out of bed? Everybody is going to know you have a hangover. You are a hopeless case!'

'You wouldn't have that bruise if you hadn't drunk so much. You made such a fool of yourself last night. OMG, what is your problem!'

DO YOU HAVE TALKING SCALES?

'You fat cow, you've put on two pounds – you are never going to lose weight because you drink too much.'

'If you could only stop drinking, you'd stop eating all those crisps.'

OUR PROTECTION AGAINST FEELING VULNERABLE

The Inner Critic is the part of our brain that monitors our fight or flight response. It is this inner language that triggers the amygdala. Now I am going to delve deeper into this science and give you the psychological aspect of it.

Many scientists believe we have had this personality trait since the cavemen days when there were potential bears around every corner, so our brain would forewarn us. I think it is fair to say that unless you live in a country where bears live, this primitive part of the brain is not helpful like it used to be.

Ironically, the Inner Critic is an important part of our thinking and responding process. The problem is it gets too much air time, an inner commentary that is detrimental to our hopes and dreams, which exacerbates the drinking issue.

The Inner Critic's role is to protect you from anxiety, stress, loneliness, fear and anger, to name a few. It thinks that if it gets in first to forewarn you about potential scary moments, you will be safe. Without realising it, we become fearful of this voice and in a nanosecond the brain will demand alcohol.

THE IMPOSTER SYNDROME: CATHERINE'S STORY

By the time Catherine came to see me, she was full of fear and self-doubt about whether she needed to go to Alcoholics Anonymous or just stop drinking altogether. Her story is a very common one that I hear a lot in my clinic work.

Catherine told me about her stressful work life, which was clearly creating a lot of anxiety. She worked in her family business and had done so since she left school. It was simply assumed she would take over when her parents retired. When I asked her if she was happy working in the family business she replied, 'No, and I feel trapped because I don't want to let my parents down, so I just have to keep going. I feel I don't have any choice but to keep working in the business because I am not qualified to do anything else!'

As Catherine continued to talk, I realised how strong her Inner Critic was and the connection to her work and over-drinking.

I explained to her that when someone is living a life that they feel they didn't choose or that they don't have a connection to or interest in, the Inner Critic starts to stir. The Inner Critic was clearly playing games with Catherine suggesting that the 'real' outside world of employment wouldn't want her because she hadn't gone through the traditional channels to find employment. The Inner Critic was driving Catherine to drink in unhelpful ways.

The Imposter Syndrome is a classic sign of someone who feels they are faking their life. In Catherine's situation, this was true. Her Inner Critic suggested that if she had have gone for an interview at her parents' company, she wouldn't have got the job. Her Inner Critic continued to hound her that the truth would be exposed to the outside world.

Catherine's professional self-esteem was low. My gut feeling was that once Catherine's confidence was worked on, it would naturally reduce the Inner Critic's commentary. Once this was achieved she would see her world in a different light.

One of her biggest fears was driven by her guilt-laden thoughts about having a drink before she got to work at 9 a.m. She had been on many websites about people with alcohol issues, which suggested if you think about drinking in the morning then you are showing signs of alcoholism. As I explained to Catherine, she didn't have a drinking problem but rather an Inner Critic issue.

The anxiety from the Inner Critic started from the moment she woke up in the morning. She admitted she was bored, angry, scared and unfulfilled but didn't know what else to do.

It was no surprise to me why Catherine's drinking had got out of hand. She was unhappy and empty within because she felt her life was not her own. Drinking was a great way to escape this.

With the work we did together in hypnosis and the Hypnosis Hub recording she listened to, she started to feel happier within. After a few weeks, Catherine's whole demeanour changed and her drinking decreased dramatically. Without the Inner Critic badgering her, some light optimistic thoughts about what she was good at started to show up. She made a decision to study part-time and go to a business school to gain her confidence. This led to more enjoyment in her workplace, as she started to contribute to the family business in more inspiring ways.

SELF-FULFILLING PROPHECY

The good news is that the Inner Critic cannot see into your future, but it will try and trick you into believing that it can. It is brilliant at playing games with you and will bring up memories from your history about your over-drinking as a mental reference.

Let me repeat this because it is really important.

The Inner Critic does not have a crystal ball; it just pretends it does. This is because it is worried you will make the same mistakes of drinking too much like before, and of course you do!

It literally uses your memory bank of each time you have drunk too much, so when you say yes to that party or have a special evening out, it will remind you like a thunderbolt about how much you have drunk in the past.

You start to feel anxious and then before you know it you need a drink to calm you down. And this is even before the event happens! This is because the Inner Critic has convinced your mind that this is what will happen, and so it does!

Sadly, it then becomes a self-fulfilling prophecy, where your mind gives in and lets the Inner Critic take over.

SILENT BUT VIOLENT

Fortunately, most of the time the world around you are not aware of your radio-crazy conversations and if people really knew how hard you were on yourself they would be shocked!

I believe the Radio-crazy Syndrome is at epidemic proportions. So if you resonate with this theory, rest assured you are far from alone. A lot of people think it is just them who doesn't like themselves, but this is far from true. The Inner Critic claims that 'everybody else has got their act together except you!'

This is instrumental in keeping people in a bad emotional space. Drinking is a great way to escape it, until the morning when you wake feeling awful with negative thoughts from the Radio-crazy Syndrome booming in your head.

This inner, unhelpful commentary affects your self-esteem and true confidence. It is also the catalyst to depression and anxiety. It is the biggest driver to plastic surgery, short-lived gym memberships and negative relationships.

The Inner Critic loves you feeling bad, because it thinks you will then be prepared for the worst-case scenario – better safe than sorry – but it has no connection to the truth whatsoever.

It knows everything about you, from your weird sexual thoughts to the cellulite on your thighs, and it will remind you of this as you are about to attempt an intimate relationship.

The Inner Critic will hinder the best-made plans to get that new job or initiate a new opportunity for you because it tells you failure is highly likely.

It will remind you of every scenario of your drinking history that intimidates you, so you feel bound by its threats and lose all your faith in your ability to drink in a healthier way.

Alcohol is the quickest way to shut down the Inner Critic.

Did you know that drinking alcohol is one of the fastest and most effective ways of shutting this negative voice down?

Did you know that your drinking relationship is nothing to do with you but is a direct response to shutting down the critical part of your brain?

So, it is no surprise that someone who worries about their drinking will keep drinking to get some relief from the Inner Critic. We use alcohol as a way to shut down this inner voice and find some peace.

Your brain genuinely thinks alcohol is the right medicine for you for that particular moment to get some space in your head.

And it works really well, until the next morning when the Inner Critic starts up again. Then the brain and body feels vulnerable and before you know it they demand you have a drink that day even though you may have promised yourself you wouldn't. As I always say with the Inner Critic, you are damned if you do and you are damned if you don't.

You need to learn to manage the Inner Critic rather than let it manage you.

RATING YOUR INNER CRITIC

Rarely (1), about average (3), frequently (5) – add up your scores at the end and see the key below for your personal Inner Critic score.

QUESTIONS	1, 3 or 5
1. I wake in the night worried about what I did yesterday.	
2. I panic about what I might have said or should have said after a few drinks.	
3. I feel everybody else is more successful than me.	
4. When I'm in company, I worry what friends, colleagues and acquaintances are thinking of me.	
5. I procrastinate on a regular basis.	
6. I am always putting myself down.	
7. I feel better socially after I have had a few drinks.	
8. I drink to suppress my Inner Critic.	
9. I wish I had more self control when it comes to drinking.	
10. When I look in the mirror, I don't like what I see.	
11. I worry that people find me boring without a drink.	
12. I feel boring unless I have had a few drinks.	
13. If people really knew me they wouldn't like me.	
14. I feel vulnerable around people who choose not to drink.	
15. I get angry when I can't say no to having a drink.	
16. I question my decisions after they have been made and worry whether I have done the right thing.	

17. When I say no I feel guilty.	
18. When I take a questionnaire like this, I'm sure that everyone else would do better than me.	
19. I avoid taking risks if I can help it.	
20. When I think about all the things I should have done, I feel I have wasted my life.	

KEY TO THE STRENGTH OF YOUR INNER CRITIC:

25–44 WEAK. Congratulations, your Inner Critic is well in check. Your self-esteem is generally healthy and anxiety is low about drinking alcohol. When you do drink you don't usually feel guilty and you have good references of drinking in moderate ways. Your drinking is more a habit than emotionally triggered.

45–74 MEDIUM. Your Inner Critic is strong in certain areas of your life. It could be that in your personal world you don't drink that much but perhaps professionally you drink more than you would truly like to, or vice versa. Your score also suggests that you have a little mistrust in your ability to drink in healthy ways and can over-drink in certain situations.

75+ STRONG. Your Inner Critic plays havoc with your emotional wellbeing and often causes overpowering guilt and unnecessary bouts of low self-worth. Anxiety and depression are more common and can encourage heavy drinking as a way to deal with life.

The Inner Critic doesn't like change because it works on history and will continue to repeat this behaviour until you give your mind new memories. The recordings will help you to do this.

THE HEALTHY CONFIDENT YOU

The good news is there is another part to you that is the opposite to the Inner Critic.

I call this part the Healthy Confident You. It is the inner voice that convinced you to read this book. It is the area of your brain that I talked about in the first chapter. It is your prefrontal cortex, that is, the executive decision-maker that knows how to keep you safe without the need of alcohol. It is the part that knows you can learn to drink less. So ignore any of your Inner Critic's comments such as 'You will fail' or 'This book won't work for you like it does for others' and don't worry. By the end of this chapter you will be ready to listen to your first recording.

I am going to show you the most effective way of training your brain to tune out the Inner Critic and tune into this intuitive part. The Healthy Confident You is such an empowering voice. In the past it didn't get enough air play, but now it can. You can train your brain to let this part be more vocal, so you can be more authentically who you are, rather than who the Inner Critic thinks you should be.

I am not suggesting you will be the happiest person on the planet every day, but I am here to let you know that feeling safe and calm about your life is a habit you can learn.

The domino effect is that you won't have this drive to drink to run away from the Inner Critic. There won't be this feeling that life is challenging, even when challenging moments occur.

What I find amazing about training your mind and body to communicate from this intuitive space is the freedom of feeling more at peace. There isn't that radio-crazy chatter going on as much or as often.

CLASSIC FM

When my drinking clients realise the true potential of who they are rather than who the Inner Critic thinks they should be, it opens up a whole world of possibilities.

When the Radio-crazy Syndrome stops, the brain can then welcome Classic FM. From this space you can naturally tune into feelings of being comfortable with who you are in lovely sober ways.

Can you imagine what it feels like to wake up in the morning without the Inner Critic berating you even before you start your day? You will know that your inner dialogue is supportive rather than restrictive.

Your mind can learn anything if you give it the space and the time. In just twenty-five minutes you will be training your brain and body to know that the Inner Critic has no foundation. It has simply been using old references and patterns of thought that are becoming out of date. You will start to notice that what the Inner Critic says about you and drinking is an old opinion.

When your mind learns to be more present with the Healthy Confident You, you will recognise that life is easier and good moments are safer to experience. You don't have to live your life on high alert to ward off potential new threats. You logically decide how and when to respond to life from a much more calm and centred space before you consume alcohol.

DECISIONS ARE EASIER

Without the doom and gloom of the Inner Critic hovering over your life, you will see opportunities that the Inner Critic squashed before. Whenever you are in an Inner Critic space it is much more difficult to make decisions, let alone the right ones.

When you are in an intuitive space, that strong sixth sense comes out and decisions are easier to make and you trust in your future. When you are in an intuitive space you don't have that drive to drink as quickly and with the same intensity, because you don't feel the need to run away from your Inner Critic through alcohol.

After using the tools in this book, many clients tell me there isn't this inner unhelpful commentary any more about what is right and what is not right for them. There is a clarity about how to move forward in life, whether it be about resigning from a job, or knowing that something in their life just isn't serving its purpose any more.

When we listen to the Inner Critic, decisions can be harder to make; there may be a sense of confusion, anxiety and self-questioning. It's not long before procrastination sets in and a lack of confidence about what is right becomes too hard, so staying put is just easier.

Learn to manage your Inner Critic rather than letting it manage you.

The recordings are rewiring your brain to welcome more calm and peace in your life, even when you are bored, lonely or sad. Your mind will accept that while a full spectrum of emotional responses exists, many of those emotions are simply driven by the Inner Critic, not you! So often the unhelpful, vulnerable moments we experience are simply a habit attached to our Inner Critic behaviour and not based on truth or reality.

POSITIVE CHEMICAL REACTIONS

It's a simple equation: when you feel safe and logical about life, your body isn't producing the stress chemicals that it was before it demanded alcohol. Your mind will produce the good feelings that feed your body with positive chemicals such as oxytocin, serotonin and dopamine. This means you don't need to drink as much to find those chemicals, because they are already there.

IT'S IN THE BAG: PETER'S STORY

Peter and his wife were having some marital problems due to the stress of him being laid off work. Money was tight and, like many couples when both are home, personal space can be difficult to find.

They started arguing a lot, which was worrying them both but equally they didn't know what to do about it.

Peter had got into the habit of taking his laptop down to the pub at lunchtime as a way to give him and his wife some space. At first this seemed like a good idea; however, it started to increase their arguments when Peter got home.

Peter's wife became aware that going to the pub was becoming a daily ritual and she became increasingly worried that the lunchtime pub moment was getting more and more engrained into his way of life. It was also costing them money they didn't have.

It got to the stage that Peter said he loathed going home knowing his wife would be critical of his drinking time, and when he didn't go to the pub he would be extra grumpy all day.

It came to a crescendo when Peter decided to outwit his wife by saying he wasn't going to the pub but would go for a walk in the park instead. He did go for that walk but with four cans of beer in his bag.

This particular day, while sitting under a tree having his beer, his wife called to ask him to urgently rush home to help her deal with a burst pipe in the kitchen.

Peter ran home, forgetting all about the forbidden beers in his bag. After the kitchen issue was resolved, his wife spotted the cans with some alarm.

SNEAKY DRINKING

Peter had started sneaky drinking, which is very common when someone is being critical of their drinking.

I am not suggesting that his wife shouldn't be worried and say something because if you love someone you want them to know you care. Peter's wife was coming from a loving space; the problem was that Peter's Inner Critic reaffirmed this external criticism, as what she was saying validated what the Inner Critic was already telling Peter.

Ironically, suggesting someone might want to drink less doesn't stop them from drinking. It often can exacerbate the problem. They may need to drink more. The sneaky drinking sets in because the Inner Critic makes the drinker feel so guilty and out of control.

BEING OBSERVED AS A DRINKER

Peter didn't realise consciously but this inner dialogue – that he was a loser who couldn't find a job, on the slippery slope to alcoholism – created low self-worth, anxiety and depression. On one hand he knew he was drinking too much but on the other hand it was his only respite from his Inner Critic.

Peter is, like every drinker who is secretly concerned about their drinking, hyper aware of the problem. They don't need to be told. They know deep down that the issue needs to be dealt with.

The one common theme with sneaky drinking is anxiety. This anxiety comes from the Inner Critic suggesting that the person who is critical about their drinking is watching with an evil eye. The Inner Critic says, 'They are watching you drinking. You'd better behave and keep your drinking to a minimum.'

Then the drinker rebels and often drinks too much to annoy the other person. This causes more dramas and the relationship breaks down even more.

From my viewpoint, I hear about sneaky drinking a lot and I can assure you, the drinking is a secondary issue. When someone feels they are being watched while drinking, they will often find somewhere to drink alone. They are usually unaware of the high levels of anxiety in their body as they do not understand the emotional habit attached to alcohol.

Their mind will demand alcohol as a way to escape this pain. The drinker is then in the dog house again and the sneaky drinking continues. This can reassure the Inner Critic and the drinker that there is a real problem, so it can become a *bigger* problem than it really is.

Getting back to Peter ... once he realised his Inner Critic was having a field day with him, he took himself to his study instead of going to the pub, where he finally listened to the first Hypnosis Hub recording.

After the very first day of this soon-to-be ongoing routine, he told me his wife said, 'Wow, you look happy, what's going on?' Peter said, 'I feel like I've found myself again and it feels great!'

Finally he was learning to manage his Inner Critic, and he felt more confident knowing it could not hurt him any more.

EXERCISING YOUR MIND

My goal is to help you also see that your drinking is a conditioned response to the high levels of stress and anxiety that life has thrown at you. These challenges trigger our Inner Critic to be hyper-vocal and unhelpful which leads us to drink more than we would like.

Life is very rarely perfect and often when situations occur that are highly stressful we need some respite. If you use alcohol as a way to deal with life more easily, then you are doing yourself a great disservice. You are so much more than a drinker.

The Healthy Confident You is there within you. It just needs to be exercised.

Like Peter did, you can regain control and silence your Inner Critic.

Start listening to the first Hypnosis Hub recording, track 1 which is 25 minutes in length. Please see (www. georgiafoster/hypnosishub) and repeat if possible once a day. You need to be lying or sitting somewhere warm and safe. It doesn't matter if you have been drinking and it doesn't make any difference what time of day you listen to it.

My top tip is to listen to it before your first drink, to get you into a safer and happier space.

Remember: It is very normal to have a busy brain or fall asleep. It won't make a difference to the results. Just trust, the information is going in, whether you are restless or sleepy and forget what I am saying.

SOMETHING TO THINK ABOUT ...

- Your Inner Critic is not you; it's just one voice. It doesn't know your future and it never will. There are a range of possible outcomes in any situation. Your Inner Critic doesn't have a hotline to the future.

- Let the Healthy Confident You be more present in your daily life.

- Without your Inner Critic degrading you, there is choice and freedom in how you want to drink.

- Sneaky Drinking is the sign of a strong internal and external critic about your drinking. When you are more present from an intuitive space, you make healthier decisions and this includes drinking less.

- When you are in a calmer and more logical place, you aren't driven to drink with the same intensity.

CHAPTER 3

THE PLEASER

WHO IS THE PLEASER?

Whenever I introduce the Pleaser to clients and workshop participants, I notice awkward smiles appear on many faces and I can identify with these awkward smiles, for the Pleaser is one that is close to my own heart. It was, and still is, one of the strongest parts of my personality. On the positive side, I have to say thanks to my Pleaser for being my front of house maître d', because it led me to this profession. However, the negative side of my Pleaser led me to many years of self-loathing and crazy, heavy drinking!

You can spot a Pleaser a mile away because they are always willing to do things that often other people are not, going the extra mile for friends, colleagues – anyone.

- Do you over-commit to keep everybody happy?
- Do you feel guilty if you say no to people?

- Do you play over in your mind what you previously said, worrying that you might have offended someone?

- Do you keep a conversation going to avoid silences?

- Do you worry about not being liked?

- Do you have a lot of acquaintances?

- Are you the social secretary for your friends?

- Do you drink to communicate?

- Do friends dump their problems on to you, knowing that you will be prepared to help out and pick up the pieces?

- If somebody does something awful to you, do you say it's OK when really you want to give them a piece of your mind?

THE FEAR OF NOT BEING LIKED

The Pleaser is the part within us that harbours the fear of not being good enough or liked enough, and this is a reflection of low self-worth. Pleasers make up a lot of my client base. If you are a Pleaser, you will notice that you spend a lot of time worrying about looking after other people to the detriment of your own health and wellbeing.

Pleasers are constantly checking in with people to make sure they are OK, rather than checking in with themselves, because they don't see themselves as important enough. They constantly undervalue themselves and overvalue the needs of the people around them.

The purpose of the Pleaser is to keep everybody else happy. The Pleaser personality is often charming, open and warm to the outside world. It can be a very attractive character trait to have, because you will be well liked. The downside is the more you look after someone else, the less time you have to look after you and this is when alcohol can become an issue.

PLEASERS ARE OFTEN CARERS

Many Pleaser clients who are the natural nurturer for their families, whether they are the main carer of children or elderly parents or relatives, can use alcohol as a form of self-care. I know how stressful this situation can be and the truth is – there is very little time for them.

Alcohol can be seen to be a way to have that time, as a quick route to self-care. In my experience, though, using alcohol for this purpose inhibits people from finding other ways to self-care that can be much more rewarding. I respect that time might be an issue, but drinking takes up a lot of time too!

I often ask Pleaser clients, if you had the time what would you do for yourself? Make a list and start to implement one or more new measures, even on a small scale. This could be treating yourself to a takeaway, running a bath instead of having a shower, or meeting a friend for a coffee. Taking time to look after yourself truly helps sober self-esteem, which will in turn help to reduce the Inner Critic's voice when it is not needed.

PLEASERS ARE POPULAR PEOPLE

Pleasers go out of their way to make sure everyone has a drink and that anybody who looks like they are being left out will be nurtured with attention. Everybody loves the party Pleaser. You will have a lot of invitations to different functions because you fill the silences at dinner parties. You encourage self-esteem in others and you will drink with them to make them feel better about themselves, even if you don't want to.

Pleasers are good listeners and will always entertain the idea of helping to co-ordinate other people's lives because they need to feel useful. The shame of it is that by keeping busy pleasing others, Pleasers have no time left energetically or emotionally for pleasing themselves.

THE WORD 'NO'

Most people love having a Pleaser in their lives, because they are prepared to do the things the other person doesn't like doing. Pleasers say yes to everything because they are frightened that if they say no, they will be rejected. The irony of this is, deep down, the fear of being rejected is more important to the Pleaser than the person they are trying to please. If you consider saying no, your internal Pleaser might tell you, 'That person will be offended' or 'if you don't say yes, they may not ask you again and then you will have lost a friend.'

The word 'no' stirs too many fearful emotions in the Pleaser; feelings of rejection, abandonment and being left out.

FRAN'S STORY

Fran was a classic Pleaser who was constantly running herself ragged with invites from her wide range of eclectic friends. She loved being popular but equally it meant a lot of boozy nights out that were starting to take their toll on her health and wellbeing.

On our first appointment together Fran told me how most of her social life revolved around alcohol and most nights there was always someone to have a drink or two with after work. I was getting a strong feeling that Fran had issues about not being liked. I asked Fran, 'Do you like going out every night?' She replied, 'Not always. I find it very stressful to have to talk and entertain and be happy all the time. Alcohol really helps me do this. If I wasn't drinking I would want to be on my own much more.'

Fran's Pleaser held her to emotional ransom with statements such as 'If you say no, they will reject you and you won't be invited out any more!' Fran believed this to be true, which kept her in a state of constant fear. She believed that if she didn't keep up with her social friends she would end up lonely.

Fran's biggest issue was that she couldn't say 'no' to drinking because she was worried that people would think she was boring and anti-social, so she kept drinking way too much when she went out to ensure her sense of belonging.

People loved Fran because she was the party girl who kept everyone together. Fran went on to say, 'Sometimes all I want to do is go home knowing I have had enough to drink, but I feel guilty if I leave before others, so I keep drinking.'

PLEASERS AND MONEY IN ABUNDANCE

Pleasers often spend money on other people because it is a way of being liked and respected. Unfortunately, they do this because they don't respect themselves enough and can find themselves being short of money. Sometimes they pay for other people's meals and buy Scrooge people drinks in the false belief that this will make the other person feel better. The reality is that Scrooge people love having Pleasers in their lives because the Pleaser usually pays the bill!

Fran told me her debt situation was way out of control and this really worried her. She would often get the bill because other people kept talking about how worried they were about money. When the truth came out we had a bit of an 'aha' moment about what was really going on. There were many friends in much better financial situations than Fran. Nevertheless, this was not enough to stop Fran from getting her credit card out too often to pay for other people's drinks.

LOW SELF-ESTEEM

If you have a strong Pleaser trait you will likely have low self-esteem and it will be reflected in overdoing things for other people so you can avoid looking at yourself. For when you do look at yourself you often see a person who is useless or a failure.

'If people really knew me they wouldn't like me' is a true Pleaser statement and it comes in all shapes and sizes, from homemakers, golfing pros through to lawyers and doctors. The Pleaser lives in all strata of our society.

WHEN THE BELL RINGS

The Pleaser has a strong sense of when to stop drinking. They know when it's time to stop. There is an internal bell that rings to say enough is enough; however, it is not strong enough in certain social situations and can often be overridden. The bell is ignored in favour of drinking to keep others happy. Pleasers feel guilty about ruining the party mode by saying no, I've had enough. They will be easily coerced into drinking far more than planned, so they can wake up in the morning knowing that they didn't let anyone down.

SOPHIE'S STORY

Sophie was working in the TV industry where long hours were expected and a lot of meetings were held in one of the many bars in Soho, London.

One morning after a heavy night out with her colleagues, her boyfriend said he had had enough of her late-night drinking and gave her an ultimatum. He asked her to come home earlier more often or else he was going to call off the relationship.

This led to a difficult situation for Sophie who was a strong Pleaser. The question she had to ask herself was, 'Do I please my boyfriend or my heavy-drinking colleagues and boss?' Ultimately her colleagues won and the relationship broke up.

When Sophie realised that her Pleaser had encouraged the heavy drinking and understood the demand of this personality trait, she felt more confident to improve her sober self-esteem. Sophie wanted to get her life in a healthier space. She listened to her Hypno Blast in the toilet before she went out with her colleagues, so she was in the zone to say 'no' to the third drink and sipped water instead. Her DOWO technique was working well and her self-esteem went through the roof.

Sophie emailed me some months later to tell me how one colleague had openly admired her new drinking behaviour. He became a client too!

PLEASERS ATTRACT BULLIES

Be careful: needy people love Pleasers because they listen and they drink. Pleasers often attract bullies as friends and partners. What a great set-up this is for many needy and emotionally demanding people!

One of the more painful parts of my work is when I know a client or seminar participant has classic Pleaser signs and has a bully as a partner. I know it will be a tricky path, as they have often been in a quagmire of an unsupportive relationship dynamic for a long time. They may know the relationship is unhelpful to their self-esteem but find it too frightening to move on.

Bullies are like magnets to a Pleaser person. Bullies love having friendships and intimate relationships with Pleasers because they get away with such bad behaviour.

Typical conversations from a bully to a Pleaser are: 'You're unlikely to get that job, I wouldn't attempt it. Other people are better qualified than you.' Or 'I wouldn't wear that dress, it doesn't flatter you.' Bullies are very good at bringing a Pleaser down and, of course, a Pleaser believes this negative conversation because they have low self-worth.

Pleasers would never speak to anybody that way because they are always so kind to people. So they live in the false belief that this person must be telling the truth.

Bullies also have the low self-worth of a Pleaser because they themselves have very low self-esteem, but it translates very differently for them. Bullies hide their lack of confidence by acting over-confidently, often bragging about their achievements and big-noting themselves to their partner and friends.

Behind closed doors, a bully can be cruel and emotionally abusive with the goal of keeping the Pleaser in a low self-esteem place. This allows them to maintain a relationship where they can hide their fears about being found out of being unhappy with who they are.

If there are any signs of the Pleaser gaining confidence they will try anything to get them back into the 'small' space the bully wants them to stay in. They may attempt to stop the Pleaser connecting to loving family members and good, long-standing friends. For they know these people can see their true colours, and therefore will demand the relationship to stop.

I see this so many times in my clinic work and it breaks my heart.

BLAMING ALCOHOL: PAT'S STORY

Many years ago, a client called Pat came to see me after her partner suggested she drank too much. I am smiling while I write this because a lot of bullies love criticising their partner about their drinking because it makes them feel even more in control of their relationship. The bad news for the bully is the drinking is not the problem; it's the low self-esteem!

Pat didn't tell her partner about our time together, which I was relieved about. Once a bully finds out a

Pleaser is seeking help, they can often panic because they are worried they will be found out to be a bully. When this happens the Pleaser can start to see the true situation and will attempt to change the dynamics or try and get out of the relationship.

Pat's partner told her she was overweight, boring, unsexy and that no one else would be interested in her. Among many other awful things he said to her, her life was full of anxieties and drinking was a great way to run away from them.

Pat said her partner used to get so angry at her but after a few drinks she didn't care and gave back as good as she could give him. He constantly berated her about this 'drinking' behaviour because she only challenged him after a bottle of wine had been consumed.

Now, this is where I defend alcohol. Some people may choose to blame alcohol's addictive personality, but I've got a very different opinion. It's not the alcohol, but rather the Inner Critic shutting down and the Pleaser starting to have some air time, telling some home truths.

The Pleaser gains confidence without the Inner Critic guarding their behaviour and often aggressive conversations start. This is common with Pleasers because alcohol affects judgement, giving them a green light to vent their built-up resentment. The problem is, they wake up in the morning with an awful pit in their stomach about what they said and what trouble they will be in now!

So my first goal with Pat was to ask her to have those difficult and challenging conversations with her bullying partner with a cup of tea in her hand, not a glass of wine. By making this one simple change, her partner could not blame the wine but acknowledge that Pat was speaking from an assertive, sober place.

It was the one step that made her partner go crazy wondering where her self-esteem was coming from. He couldn't figure it out until one day he went looking through her phone and found an email from me with a link to her personalised recording.

He emailed me to say I was not addressing her alcohol issues and that she would not be coming back to see me, and sadly he was right. I never saw her again.

PLEASING YOURSELF TO HAVE SOBER COMMUNICATION

When a person begins to work with their Pleaser it can have an interesting effect, which could be likened to throwing a pebble into a lake. Through this action, circles radiate out and relationship dynamics can change. You need to crawl before you can walk and take baby steps, one at a time.

The strong, small steps could simply be telling the man in the local shop who short-changed you that you noticed it and you want your money back. Or it could be that you say no to a demanding friend who has a bullying nature. The rewards are endless.

How long can you keep saying yes to everyone? Will it be when you go bankrupt? Or perhaps have an emotional breakdown? That's when you will see who is truly around for you.

One of the key aspects of my work is to build sober self-esteem, so healthier communication can take place and people know where they stand with you.

I don't know how many clients come to see me because there was 'that' moment where they said something they truly regretted after drinking that broke down good family and relationship dynamics. Perhaps it took years to build those solid foundations with your in-laws, banished in one angry alcohol-fuelled exchange.

Sober communication takes practice. From my experience it is the only way for a Pleaser's voice to be heard and taken seriously. As soon as alcohol is involved it will dilute and/or dismiss your opinion and this is not fair on the Pleaser or the relationship.

Sober, healthy communication takes practice, which is where the Hypnosis Hub recordings can help.

WHITE LIES

Sometimes you will need to avoid certain people for a while, which means the 'little white lie' theory comes into play – a small lie that is told to avoid upsetting another person. I don't like lies at the best of times, but for a Pleaser this is a must until they gain more sober confidence to say 'no'.

Choose who you want to spend time with and who you don't want to see. Who makes you feel good about yourself, and who do you often feel uncomfortable with?

In order to build your successful software of learning how to please the Healthy Confident You, tell friends that due to unexpected work commitments you are going to have to lay off the alcohol. People will sympathise. Message the ones you don't want to see or email so that you don't have to discuss why you have made this decision. It's your business how you want to spend your time, nobody else's.

PLEASERS' OWN PROBLEMS

Pleasers are not always keen on expressing how they feel about their lives to other people. The Pleaser finds this uncomfortable, because if other people know they are vulnerable then they may not be there to please them. No one likes to be thought of as a drag, after all. Pleasers are always saying they are fine, and yet most of the time they are not. They are drowning in their own low self-esteem because they do not value their needs as much as other people's. This low self-worth leads to moodiness and the desire to hibernate from the outside world. Pleasers need to retreat from time to time, simply to recharge their batteries, and drinking alone is a way of achieving this.

Pleasers will enjoy the 'solo party' moments where they can kiss the world goodnight, and sit down and drink. As I mentioned earlier in the book, there is nothing wrong with drinking on your own, but the goal is to do so from a positive space – and not because you want to numb yourself.

For many Pleasers it is their time to take a break from the demands of the outside world, where they don't have to be doing this or that to help others. It can also be a place where they are alone with their own negative feelings.

The slippery slope of drinking too much during this time can occur as their tolerance of alcohol goes up. While in this quiet space a Pleaser (because they don't want to burden others with their problems) may fester and become angry and mad at the world because they feel unheard. Pleasers can harbour bitterness towards people in their lives who don't seem to care for them back. Their communication with themselves is poor because of the presence of the Inner Critic, which continues to stimulate negative thinking. On the other hand a Pleaser may relish this time, a positive space to have a solo party that is about taking time out and watching a great movie or listening to music.

Whatever the solo drinking situation is about, it is fine

to drink alone, but the alcohol does need to be monitored as before you know it that half bottle is gone and another one is being opened.

Try one of the Hypnosis Hub recordings before you have that solo party. This will get you into a good, calm space before drinking.

ILL-HEALTH

Pleasers don't tend to get sick very often. When a Pleaser is ill they cannot look after other people, so they avoid getting ill at all costs. However, when they do call in sick, they do it well. Being ill is the only socially acceptable method of gaining instant sympathy.

They might even be hypochondriacs, always having a worse disease than you because, in their unconscious mind, this is the only legitimate way of accepting attention.

Much has been written about the mind–body connection. Illness can be a safety mechanism to release the anxiety the Pleaser has physically stored in his or her body. Being ill is also a time out tool from the anxiety the Pleaser creates.

MIND READER

The Pleaser within us is often intuitive to other people's needs. Like the Inner Critic, the Pleaser also thinks it can read other people's minds and, to a certain extent, it can. A Pleaser has become so adept at picking up on other people's problems that they become the crystal-ball reader, assuring people that everything is going to turn out alright for them.

On the flip side is that over a period of time, the Pleaser can become irritated that other people cannot read their mind in return. This can stew inside them. The build-up of a long-standing situation can lead to a complete outburst of rage, and when a Pleaser blows you don't want to be anywhere near because it's like Mount Etna!

This can happen in a sober state, which will shock friends and family, as they realise something is actually really wrong.

ASKING FOR HELP

If you are a Pleaser, asking for help is a big issue. You are great at saying yes to everyone else, but opening up to your own problems and sharing them is unacceptable because it is scary. This is because the Pleaser is worried that if people knew their fears and vulnerabilities they wouldn't want to hang around them any more. They fear that these people will not be understanding and think they are weak in nature and possibly appear slightly unhinged emotionally. Pleaser's do not want to appear emotionally unstable because they want to be the stability for other people in their lives.

Friends and family may not be in the habit of asking if a Pleaser is alright because they generally get the same answer: 'I'm fine'. Is it any wonder that after a while people stop asking a Pleaser how s/he is?

THE ASSERTIVE, POSITIVE PLEASER

The Pleaser part in you has so much to offer the world. Its genuine desire for kindness, warmth, fairness and unconditional love can benefit you too. It just takes practice.

If you look at all the qualities the Pleaser has to offer everybody else, you can see for yourself what a wonderful asset it could be for yourself. Imagine if you started to nurture yourself a little more without alcohol in your bloodstream?

At this point you may experience a little bit of unease stirring inside you because the Pleaser might be concerned that if you look after yourself then other people will reject you. For example, you may choose not to see so much of friends who tend to air their problems at great length when you get together.

Or you might decide not to take your children away on that full-on activity holiday if you don't have the energy for it yourself. It is normal for a Pleaser to feel this way and I would be surprised if you didn't have any stirrings.

In fact, if you do not have any stirrings, then congratulations – you do not have a strong Pleaser! Training your

Pleaser to spend time out looking after you can be stressful and a little testing, but the people who care about you will get used to it and you will too. If someone doesn't like you saying no or taking time out, then the relationship clearly is not a supportive one and you may need to change it anyway. This process is like starting a new relationship, but this time it is with yourself.

The net effect is that you won't need to drink too much to communicate, or feel the need to belong by drinking to please others.

HOW THE PLEASER CAN WORK WITH YOU RATHER THAN AGAINST YOU

What a pleasure it is to look after people with the knowledge that caring is your own choice, rather than triggered by the fear of others' rejection. The good news is that having a Pleaser personality means that you will always be interested in other people and the world around you. Pleasers love exploring new ideas partly because this aids them in their conversations with others and giving advice.

I have a story I often share with seminar participants about a client of mine who has sent many people to see me.

STACEY'S STORY

Stacey was the high-level manager of a bank. She was single and partied very hard with her colleagues and friends.

She came to see me about her stress levels. After learning more about her life it was evident her alcohol consumption was concerning. She would generally start with a few cocktails and then have a bottle and half of wine, and then when she got home she would always have a nightcap of Irish whiskey.

I asked her if she had any hardcore-drinking friends and her reply was, 'Loads. Everyone drinks a lot in my life.' I could tell Stacey was a Pleaser, so I stipulated that between our first and next appointment she avoid any heavy-drinking bullying friends for a few days. This was with the goal to build her confidence up about drinking to please herself rather than others. She was really uncomfortable with this, as she had planned to meet one of these friends that evening. I said, 'Tell her a little white lie, while you please me for this moment.' Which she finally agreed to do.

The next week, Stacey walked in, sat down and burst into tears. I am not a psychic but I quickly figured out what she was going to say. 'Georgia I have failed you,' she said. 'I promised you I wouldn't see any of my heavy-drinking friends this past week but I caved in last night and got horribly drunk with one of them. I am so angry at myself because I drank way too much and even more than normal. I must be one of your hopeless clients!'

I assured her this was not the case. It simply confirmed how strong her Pleaser was and how much it was hindering her quality of life while she continued to drink to please others.

She told me the full story. Stacey was running late after a meeting. Rather than take the train because her friend didn't like being kept waiting (but always kept Stacey waiting), Stacey decided to take a taxi, which ended up taking twice as long as there was a terrible traffic jam. By the time Stacey arrived at the venue, she was flustered but felt proud of herself as she had rehearsed her 'drink less chat' in the taxi. She jumped out feeling confident, ready to meet her bullish friend with her assertive request, 'No need to buy a whole bottle of wine, let's just go by the glass as I have a big meeting tomorrow.'

Stacey went to the toilet and on the way back could see from a distance that her friend had purchased a whole bottle of wine. She felt angry and unheard. I asked her what happened next. 'I heard all about my friend's family dramas, boyfriend rejections and money issues and oh I ended up paying the bill! You see Georgia, I have absolutely failed you and I feel terrible.'

I told her she hadn't let me down at all. Instead what she had just shown me was how much of her life was about pleasing others to the detriment of herself.

Do you regularly see friends who complain about their lot in life? That's fine, as long as it's not always your friend who is doing most of the talking and the moaning. Think about the percentage of time that you generally spend offloading your own worries – is it small in comparison? Do you think your friend might privately label you a failure or a bore if you talked about your own concerns? Many Pleasers will turn to alcohol to get through an evening of dutiful listening.

YOU HAVE A CHOICE

Being free to express what you want to say means that there is no mind-reading going on. People are relieved when you tell them what you want, because it makes it easier for them, not more difficult. It also means that you will be able to have healthier relationships with the people around you without having to get drunk to express yourself. The beauty of this is you will be able to achieve more because you have expressed to them what you want when you are sober.

The alternative to not saying what you want to another person means you come home frustrated that somebody else has dominated the agenda yet again. Then there is that potential glass of alcohol to offset your anger.

Having the freedom to be able to do what you want to do means you won't feel the need to push down your feelings through the use of alcohol. Therefore, you will feel more in control of your life. This should result in an increase in self-esteem and healthier relationships with the people around you.

Embrace your inner Pleaser as a wonderful part of you that now knows it is safe to be a little selfish with your time and your energy, so you can develop the self-belief to enhance your life and future. Your world will blossom and so will you!

PRACTICE PRIVATELY

One of the best ways to introduce your assertive Pleaser is to rehearse privately at home. For example, if you have a difficult relationship with your boss and perhaps you feel unable to express how you feel, start to rehearse the conversation in your mind first. Remember to take baby steps; this way you will gradually gain confidence. The best time to do this is while listening to the Hypnosis Hub recordings. While listening to the recordings, use all of your senses. The repetition is simply going to affirm that pleasing yourself is a safe and normal experience. At home, or somewhere where you can simply be with yourself, go over and over in your mind what you want to say in a kind but definite way. Other people say what they really want to say – why shouldn't you?

SOMETHING TO THINK ABOUT ...

- It's time to please you rather than the heavy-drinking world around you.

- You are your priority, so any unhelpful relationships that hinder your sense of self-worth need to adapt to the true you.

- Becoming assertive is a win/win situation for you and others as your voice is heard and people become more respectful to you.

- Sober communication means not needing to drink to express what you want to say.

CHAPTER 4

THE PERFECTIONIST

- Are you good at alcohol-free days, weeks or months?

- Are you a binge-drinker?

- Are you or do you aspire to be a high achiever?

- Do you trust yourself with your alcohol consumption?

- Do people around you think of you as a binge-drinker?

- Do people who love you worry about how much you drink?

- Do you justify your binge-drinking by having lots of alcohol-free days?

THE ALL-OR-NOTHING DRINKER

There is no one-size-fits-all when it comes to drinking; and yet, there is a very strong personality trait that plays a major part when it comes to over-consumption of alcohol. The easiest and most simple way of explaining this tricky character is to call it the Perfectionist!

It is what it says on the can. A personality trait that is driven to be 100 per cent good at doing certain things, and this includes binge-drinking or not drinking at all.

Some time ago, a guy on one of my seminars shook his head periodically throughout the morning, and then when I talked about the Inner Critic, the Pleaser and the connection to the amygdala he appeared irritated. It was quite unnerving. As a public speaker, sometimes there are people in the audience who rattle me, and he was one of them.

Even his body language was defensive. He moved around a lot in his seat and looked agitated. It got to the point that the people sitting either side, as well as behind him, started to look agitated too. So I made a decision to chat with him in the lunch break to find out why he was behaving this way, and how we could rectify this.

Fortunately I didn't need to have that conversation with him because as soon as I started talking about the Perfectionist personality, his whole persona changed. He looked totally engrossed in what I had to say and that's when I knew he was a Perfectionist!

This man put his hand up at the end and said, 'Georgia, I've been sitting here all morning thinking I'm in the wrong place today. I was ready to leave at lunchtime. I don't want to sound cocky but I don't have self-esteem issues. In fact, I don't have any stresses in my life at all. I'm a rich bloke who loves his wife, has two beautiful children and I couldn't be happier. Still, now I get it!'

BINGE-DRINKING IS THE SIGN OF A PERFECTIONIST

The Perfectionist loves to drink a lot but they are also good at alcohol-free days. They are also good at going to the gym, watching their weight and maintaining a relatively balanced life. And yet, when they do drink, they drink way too much. This is not because they want to drink too much, but because their brain and body get tired of being perfect!

Going back to the man in the seminar, he went on to explain, 'I'm a self-made man and my time is my own. I have a ritual of going to the gym every weekday at 6 a.m., then I'm at my desk by 9 a.m. and I work really hard until 6 p.m. I don't drink at all during the week, but come Friday I blitz it! I drink three bottles of wine every Friday and Saturday night, and on Sundays … it starts earlier as we normally have a Sunday roast, so I'm drinking by noon. Sundays end up being a bit of a write-off for me! It drives my wife mad and if I am truthful it drives me mad too. Until just now, I couldn't understand my drinking behaviour. You have described my drinking habit to a tee!'

This was my attendee's 'a-ha' moment. The light bulb went on and all afternoon he was so relaxed and ready to move on. I felt thrilled that he had stuck out the morning. Since then he has been kind enough to be a testimonial for my drink-less approach.

This man was a classic binge-drinker. He was brilliant at not drinking and equally brilliant at drinking!

NO SELF-TRUST

This is the key issue with Perfectionists: they don't trust themselves with alcohol. Their justification and reprieve is to not drink. They have lots of alcohol-free days as a way to make themselves feel better.

This denial mentality gets them into a lot of trouble, not just with themselves, but in their relationships.

Typical comments from family members include, 'Maybe you should quit drinking because you just can't seem to drink in a "normal" fashion.' Then the Perfectionist panics because they feel exposed, and may not drink for months, or even years. They are worried and too proud to admit their problem because they are perfect!

EXPOSING VULNERABILITIES

The Perfectionist doesn't like to be criticised and equally doesn't like being found out. So a drinker may actually quit alcohol completely because they don't trust themselves with it.

They may choose to abstain from alcohol because they don't like feeling vulnerable, or failing. They will not like any hint of being judged or compared because they like to keep up appearances.

The Perfectionist drinker can get themselves into a 'damned if they do and damned if they don't drink' situation. They truly do want to drink in a healthier way but just can't seem to do it. So they stop drinking to alleviate the stress and strain it puts on themselves and the people around them.

'NO' IS EASY

Unlike the Pleaser personality, they are good at saying 'no' to people. They don't have any problems abstaining at birthday parties or moments of celebration if they are having an alcohol-free day. This is not because they are happy about it but rather, once again, they don't trust themselves. They make an absolute decision to not drink to take the pressure off.

A Perfectionist, unlike the Pleaser, is prepared to have confrontational conversations sober and is comfortable with being unpopular. They have their opinion and they don't care who the audience is (generally) and they can often be very set in their ways.

They might be slightly irritating to Pleasers because they can say 'no' to drinking, which annoys Pleasers. This is why Pleasers only hang out with Pleasers when they drink by choice, and only welcome Perfectionists when they are in the binge-drinking mode!

RIGHT RATHER THAN WRONG

Perfectionists often have a problem being wrong and do not like it when they are challenged. They pride themselves on knowing certain subjects and will stick to them so they do not appear ill-informed or ill-educated.

If they feel exposed, they will do their research to either back up what they believe or scurry away ashamed that they are not as perfect as they appear to be. This is often why they drink, to console themselves.

KEEPING SAFE: TAMSIN'S STORY

Going back to the seminar man, even though he said he didn't have low self-worth and felt his life was on track, I felt this wasn't actually true.

He did acknowledge after the seminar that he had an Inner Critic, and if he could only get his drinking issue sorted then his life would be perfect! Alas, life is very rarely perfect and this is where Perfectionists become undone.

Another seminar attendee, Tamsin, was a classic Perfectionist, highly driven and mad about sports. She was always well groomed and very good at making sure she was always the designated driver home during the week, because she never drank. This was her way of knowing she wouldn't succumb to drinking alcohol.

Tamsin came to see me because she had had a drinking moment that took her over the edge and it really worried her.

She went to a colleague's wedding with her husband where she had promised herself she wouldn't drink. They stayed in the hotel for the night because it was too far to drive home and, like other people from her office, she wanted to relax and enjoy the day and evening.

After a few hours Tamsin thought, 'Sod it, I am going to have a drink' and so started drinking champagne cocktails, mixed with Tequila shots and wine. Tamsin said she remembers her husband trying to curtail her drinking but doesn't remember much else after that.

She woke in the morning around 4 a.m. feeling dehydrated and disorientated because she was in a new environment from her bedroom. She looked over and saw her boss lying next to her!

MEMORY LOSS

Tamsin felt a surge of absolute terror and staggered back to her own room to find her husband asleep. He was none the wiser, but Tamsin had a full-blown alcohol-induced panic attack and started to vomit into the toilet.

Her husband woke and cursed her for being so late to bed after being such a nightmare at the wedding the night before. This panicked Tamsin even more because she didn't have any memory of the evening past 10 p.m. She desperately tried to piece together what happened but had complete memory loss.

Perfectionists understand this issue very well, which is one of the reasons why they don't like drinking that often. This is because they drink a lot of alcohol quickly and don't stop to hydrate themselves with water. The brain and body cannot keep up with the amount of alcohol and that's when the memory loss occurs.

As soon as Tamsin's husband woke, he told her she had picked a fight with him when he asked her to slow down her drinking. Rather than having a big argument, her husband decided to leave her to her drinking frenzy and go to bed.

Tamsin said she told her husband she wanted to go straight home rather than have breakfast with her colleagues because she felt ashamed by her behaviour.

They drove home in silence as Tamsin's Inner Critic and Perfectionist confirmed that her 'all or nothing' drinking had put her professional life and marriage in jeopardy.

Fortunately, Tamsin's anxiety was quickly alleviated on Monday when her boss reassured her that nothing had happened. She was so drunk that he and a colleague took her to his room because she couldn't find her key and they didn't want to wake her husband.

Tamsin's story is typical of a Perfectionist drinker. By the time she came to see me, she was convinced that she needed to stop drinking completely, as did her husband.

ANXIETY IS KEY

Tamsin's pattern of drinking had a history behind it. She had many similar stories to the wedding, which made her feel very anxious and, indeed, I got it. What Tamsin couldn't understand is why she couldn't just drink a bit too much like others at the wedding without what she called 'having a blowout'.

Blowouts, or what I call 'furiously quick drinking', are classic with the Perfectionist personality.

Tamsin's Inner Critic used her history of drinking as the reference to how she drinks. In other words, her mind scanned her drinking past and said, 'if you drink, we know what will happen, you will drink too much' and of course she did just that.

Before Tamsin decided to have her first drink, the Inner Critic was suggesting that a negative heavy-drinking moment might occur. This fired the amygdala, which triggered lots of anxiety and stress. At first she tried to ignore this anxiety. Then her body demanded that she relax in this work/social situation. She told herself, 'everybody else is drinking so why shouldn't I?' Tamsin gave in to this demand and drank too much too quickly to alleviate her earlier anxiety.

To reiterate, anxiety is key when it comes to drinking too much and too quickly. Combined with Tamsin's Perfectionist personality and her history of 'all or nothing' drinking, it is no surprise that this situation occurred.

THE BELL DOESN'T RING

For the Perfectionist, unlike the Pleaser, the bell doesn't ring when it's time to stop drinking. This is because the demands of being perfect and the inner pressure to not drink trigger a rebellious attitude. The mind almost feels desperate as the first glass of alcohol is consumed: 'Thank goodness, I don't have to be perfect now!' It's like taking a holiday from the restrictions and the 'absolutely got to get it right all the time' attitude. It's exhausting! So it is no surprise that a Perfectionist drinks the way they do.

The brain and body don't want the bell to ring because they are enjoying the freedom of not having to be responsible and attempting to achieve all of the time. So it is no surprise that a Perfectionist gets so drunk and often very quickly. It's the freedom of being in this space without the combination of the Inner Critic and the Perfectionist's expectations that sober life brings them. They want to stay in this space as long as possible, so the bell just doesn't ring.

They wake with remorse the next day, promising themselves, 'This is it! I can't do this any more. Maybe I need to go to Alcoholics Anonymous or just stop drinking!' They just can't trust themselves with alcohol.

HISTORY REPEATING ITSELF

For those who abstain for months, or even years, and then decide to drink again, it is often with the assumption that they will drink in a responsible way. They think they will be able to handle the alcohol. Frustratingly, for the drinker, this is often not the case. First, the brain and body have lost their tolerance to alcohol so they get drunk very easily and quickly. More importantly, the drinker's mind will review their drinking history, which means they tend to go back to fast and furious binge-drinking alternated with abstaining periods.

HOW HENRICK CREATED A NEW DRINKING HISTORY

Many years ago a client called Henrick called me mid-December to ask if he could book a private appointment for the first week in January. This was an unusual request, as most people like to lie pretty low for the first few weeks of the New Year. I was living in London at the time. January is a month where people tend to hibernate and many of my clients attempt Dry January as part of their New Year resolutions and abstain until the first of February.

Henrick was no exception. He had decided not to drink in January and was feeling pretty confident about it as he had done this for many previous years with great success.

I was curious as to how I could help him. Not all my clients come to me to drink less, and I wondered if he was coming about something else.

Henrick explained that he was going on a stag weekend with his best friend in the third week of January and didn't want to drink. He felt coming to see me could help him have a stronger resolve. I agreed I could help him do this, but I was more interested in his Dry January approach and how he thought he was going handle going back to drinking in February.

When Perfectionists make a decision they like to stick to it, and find it irritating if their decision is kyboshed.

Henrick was no exception. He was annoyed that his best friend wanted to have a weekend away, when he knew that Henrick didn't drink in January. Of course, they were big drinking buddies too which made Henrick anxious, but he had said to himself, 'A promise is a promise and I must stick to it.'

I asked Henrick what would happen when he returned to drinking in February. His answer was, 'I hope after not drinking for a month that I will drink less than I did before January, but [cue embarrassed chuckle] I don't drink less. I guess the bonus is not drinking for a month gives my liver a break and it has become a ritual for me and I do enjoy it once I get into it.'

IS ABSTAINING GOOD?

I agree that abstaining from alcohol is liberating for many drinkers and a good thing to do for many reasons such as liver health, sober sex, better-quality sleep and having more energy. For Perfectionists, though, it can be to the detriment of their own self-worth because when they do go back to drinking, they tend to go back to the binge cycle of drinking again and can feel quite angry at themselves.

Henrick was a Perfectionist who had trained his mind to perfect not drinking each January and he did a good job of it too. His frustration at being a Perfectionist and then going back to the old habit of drinking in unhelpful ways in February led him to some dark times. He didn't understand why he just couldn't drink less.

CREATING A NEW DRINKING RELATIONSHIP

So I said to Henrick, there are two ways we can work. One is with your original plan to deal with the heavy-drinking stag weekend by not drinking. The other is to create a new drinking/thinking habit, so you can drink alcohol while you are away on this stag weekend but without blitzing it.

Henrick shook his head and said no, this wasn't possible. 'I have to stick to my guns with this,' he said. When I explained that I thought he had a Perfectionist thinking/drinking problem and maybe he had the all-or-nothing drinking syndrome, he looked inspired.

'Maybe we could work on your mind creating new references, so that your history of drinking without the bell ringing when you have drunk too much really is your past rather than how you drink now?' I suggested.

Henrick liked this idea. His eyes lit up. This was the opportunity to change his drinking relationship with himself that could stop the shame he had been feeling.

Henrick's mind needed new mental references to tell him how he now dealt with drinking alcohol. His mind needed to learn how to have a different relationship with alcohol that wasn't a feast or famine approach. Henrick, like other Perfectionists, needed to create new neural pathways that led to the prefrontal cortex first, before the alcohol affected his thinking. When this is achieved there is a calm logic about drinking and the good news is, it can become guilt-free! Without the angst, the fear and lack of self-trust there is a greater sense of ease and there isn't a frenzy to drink in unhelpful ways.

Henrick's Perfectionist, along with his Inner Critic, stopped him from creating these new memory references simply because there wasn't any evidence of him drinking in a balanced way. It wasn't because he didn't have the resources to achieve this but rather the Perfectionist was worried he might fail, and failure doesn't work with a Perfectionist.

Henrick went on his best friend's stag weekend and he did have a few hangovers, but he said his drinking was much slower and he noticed how much more his friends drank. In fact, one of his friends tried to coerce him to drink more, but he felt this strong urge to say no, which he did. In the past, Henrick (who was known as the *big* drinker) would drink others under the table, and was the one urging others to drink too much. He came home feeling confident knowing that he had started to build healthier and more positive references. His drinking relationship had gone through a testing time, which proved to Henrick that his mind could change.

PERFECTING A DRINKING BALANCE

When a Perfectionist wants to drink less, they want to measure each glass and compare one drinking night to the next. Their expectations are high and this is part of the Perfectionist's problem. They want to drink less but worry they won't get it right and retreat back into old binge-drinking ways.

The Perfectionist needs to create the evidence of a number of successful events where they drink when they wouldn't have before. I will develop this in the last chapter so for now be reassured that if you are a Perfectionist your history of drinking does not represent your future. Your drinking style is purely a habit that can change.

The key to creating a healthier and more realistic approach is to perfect a balance, and to get that bell to ring when you know you have reached your healthy limit is really important too. This is why the Hypnosis Hub recordings are key.

It is an amazing feeling to experience a sensation of calm, instead of an uneasy sense of abandonment, before drinking, so if you resonate with the Perfectionist, there is another way forward and it starts with your amazing unconscious mind. Isn't it nice to know that you can learn to manage your alcohol rather than allow it to manage you!

SLEEP ISSUES

Perfectionists can be terrible sleepers and often use alcohol as a way to shut out the Inner Critic and the Perfectionist so that they can sleep. They worry about yesterday and why they didn't get something right or ignite fears about the future, which stops them from sleeping.

Unlike the Pleaser, who generally loves sleeping because it is a way to escape the responsibilities of looking after others, the Perfectionist has a 'busy brain' so may, on alcohol-free days, even resort to sleeping tablets or other methods to try to get to sleep.

Alternatively, some sleep really well because the Perfectionist side of their personality has worn them out emotionally.

BEING IN THE MOMENT

Either way, the Perfectionist finds it difficult to stop and just be in the moment because they are always busy driving themselves onwards to achieve more. They find it hard to be mindful because stopping to take time out means that they are not moving forward.

I know many Perfectionist clients often feel over-whelmed with the demands they make on themselves and that the only way to stop being driven is to drink alcohol. This stops the 'doing' bit of life really well, so that the

Perfectionist can then welcome the freedom of being in the moment where they can relax and just be.

This is why so many Perfectionists don't drink during the week (which is not a bad thing; I encourage alcohol-free days). However, if it is due to a lack of self-trust as regards drinking in healthier ways, it can be a problem.

Going back to my seminar man, he couldn't understand this feast or famine drinking behaviour until he understood that being in the moment was an issue for him. His mind needed the alcohol in order to 'stop and smell the roses of life'. His high-achieving mind inhibited him from relaxing because it meant he wasn't focused on building future successes. He had trained himself to always be prepared, so just hanging out and living for now made him feel unsafe. His mind had learned to save these in-the-moment situations for the weekend where he could justify drinking this way.

PERFECTIONISTS DON'T LIKE CHANGE

The Perfectionist has an issue with change, because the rigidity of their familiar drinking pattern, even if it is unhelpful drinking, is where they feel safe.

In order for the Perfectionist to change their drinking relationship, they need to learn new patterns of drinking that are calm, logical and slow-paced, without the intensity of drinking too much. Once these situations become familiar, their mind and body will accept this as being 'perfect' behaviour.

SIMON'S SLIP-UP

Often the Perfectionist client is on a high after coming to see me or after one of my seminars, because they can see first-hand how fast the results are. The downside is that one slip-up – perhaps the one night they go out with an old friend and drink more than planned – can make them question if it is working any more.

They see one slip-up as going back to square one, which is incredibly frustrating for me as a therapist. This is because I know they have created such great references, or what I often call 'evidence' of drinking less. But their Perfectionist isn't happy with this one slip-up. It wants the drinker to be consistently good at drinking perfectly.

The Perfectionist can have so many wonderful moments stored in their mind to confirm that they drink less habitually, and yet one alcohol-fuelled night can make them feel they have failed.

Simon, a classic Perfectionist client, was delighted with what we achieved together in hypnosis. He was over the moon with his 'drink less' success.

He told everyone about my special approach and then a year later I received an email from him with a very different story. He came to see me the following week.

Simon told me how well the drinking had gone for six months. He felt confident he had his drinking in check. Then one weekend he went away with some old university friends and they, as a group, drank way too much.

Simon had a blackout and couldn't remember any of the evening past 11 p.m. In the morning he was horrified to learn from his friends that he had violently vomited into the champagne bucket at the restaurant. His mind had recalled this behaviour as familiar, as this is what he used to do with these people – drink to excess.

Although it was a one-off situation, he believed he had failed and he then started to go back to the old style of all-or-nothing drinking.

Because his Inner Critic and Perfectionist were giving him such a hard time about the evening, he started to lose confidence in his ability to drink in a balanced way.

I reassured Simon he was not a hopeless case. The chain of events simply demonstrated the high expectations of his Perfectionist, and that no one is perfect, including him!

Simon agreed that he had six months of great references. His tolerance to alcohol had reduced over six months, so the increase in alcohol, as well as the extra time drinking, didn't help either. He had stopped listening to his Hypnosis Hub recordings exactly when he should have listened to them more. Simon said his Inner Critic told him not to bother with the recordings because he was too far gone and couldn't go back.

NO ONE IS PERFECT

No one is perfect, including a Perfectionist drinker. The goal is to achieve more and more positive references that reflect drinking in a slow and healthy way on a regular basis. For example, if you happen to be invited out to a big posh party and the champagne is free-flowing, so what! Life is for living. A few glasses here and there are fine, because this is a one-off situation.

The key is for the Perfectionist to continue to build positive references, so they can prove to themselves that their regular drinking is in check with the Healthy Confident You. The odd time they drink more than planned, they can see it as 'just something that happens from time to time'. The Hypnosis Hub recordings will help the Perfectionist achieve some balance to their drinking life.

COMBINATION OF BEING A PERFECTIONIST AND A PLEASER

I know some readers may feel they are a combination of a Pleaser and a Perfectionist.

Some people are Perfectionist in their professional life and yet a strong Pleaser in their personal life, and vice versa. This is very normal and is actually a good balance.

Having duality means you are a high achiever but equally do have a lot of empathy about other people and life in general. Perfectionists are not so concerned about what other people think and find it more difficult to see the other person's point of view. So when someone has a crossover between these two personalities, it can be helpful.

REBECCA'S STORY

A client called Rebecca came to see me about her white-wine drinking. Part of her role was taking clients out for dinner a few times a month. Rebecca didn't like this side of her work life but accepted it was a necessity to progress her career. She felt it was important when she organised these client dinners to drink alcohol to please the people there; even though her Perfectionist wasn't happy, her Pleaser felt it necessary.

This is where the combination of the two personalities can appear at opposite ends but actually can work really well together. Rebecca would drink red wine, which she didn't like the taste of. This would stop her from going full throttle and drinking too much with clients. She would sit on a glass of wine all night at these dinners to please others while secretly chastising herself for drinking something she didn't like during the week.

Rebecca would come home after sipping the red wine and feel like she needed to have another drink to please herself. Even if it was 11 p.m. at night, she would feel this deep desire to open up her favourite chardonnay. Knowing full well that she had to get up early didn't stop her from finishing the entire bottle. She just couldn't understand why she would do this.

Rebecca realised that her Perfectionist wanted to keep her in check in her working life by sipping red wine that she didn't like, but the Pleaser wanted her to drink, so the compromise was made. The bottle of white wine at home was the compromise and the guilt and shame drinking continued.

The goal of Rebecca and I working together was to get that balance right and for her to become assertive enough to decide she didn't need to drink at these work functions if she chose not to. Or, alternatively, if she did drink she could drink white wine and alternate with water to slow her drinking down. Rebecca perfected the DOWO (drink one water one) technique, which saved her from drinking the white wine too quickly. It also allowed her to enjoy the company at dinner and feel much more relaxed in this part of her professional life.

GETTING THE BALANCE RIGHT

Like everything in life, getting the balance right can be tricky.

Why not celebrate a wonderful midweek moment with a glass of champagne, or take that lovely walk down to the river or beach and have a glass or two on a sunny day? This is possible when you train your brain and body to be kinder to you.

If the Perfectionist gets in your way of drinking to celebrate, for example, because you've just got a job promotion and you promised yourself you wouldn't drink until the weekend, stop giving yourself a hard time. Put one of the Hypnosis Hub recordings on and get yourself into a better and safer place.

SOME THINGS TO THINK ABOUT ...

- Life is very rarely perfect. Drinking less takes practice without trying to be perfect.

- Alternate water with alcohol, so you can naturally slow your drinking down.

- Recognise that a rigid approach inhibits positive change.

- Your history of either not drinking or drinking too much is a Perfectionist personality trait that can change.

- Keep a diary to see the good moments where you drink in healthy ways, so you have the evidence of drinking less.

CHAPTER 5

THE INNER CHILD

WHAT IS THE INNER CHILD?

Every time I work with my clients, locating and connecting with their Inner Child, they experience a melting pot of emotion and feelings. To be honest with you, every time I work with my own Inner Child, I also experience powerful emotions. The most powerful feeling is to acknowledge your unique vulnerability.

The Inner Child is the part within us all that loves to play, cry, be touched and loved. It is the raw emotional state that can hold you back throughout your life because it may have been suppressed in the process of your developing into adulthood. If you had to grow up emotionally before your natural childhood age, perhaps if you were bereaved or the child of an acrimonious divorce or you grew up in a family where affection was scorned or withheld, then your Inner Child may have learned that asking for love and affection can get you into trouble. When the Inner Child becomes frightened, it hides away deep within the unconscious mind, often only making an appearance infrequently.

The Inner Child is the wonderful, loving part within all of us and the great thing about exploring your relationship with your Inner Child is that it can lead you to a much deeper and more powerful way of getting to know who you really are. Spending time exploring this part means you will become more whole in how you view yourself and the relationships around you.

The Inner Child only knows how to live and be in the present moment and this can be a difficult and intense experience for many men and women. They suppress their adult part through alcohol to free their Inner Child so they can access the freedom to joke and have fun.

The questions listed below are a reflection of the Inner Child behaviour. As you read through the questions check in with yourself as to how and when you have experienced these emotions and feelings. Do you need alcohol to feel free enough to express yourself?

ALCOHOL AND THE INNER CHILD

- When was the last time you had a real belly laugh while sober?

- When was the last time you had a really good cry while sober?

- When was the last time you wanted to be stupid while sober?

- How often do you rebel like a naughty child after drinking?

- When was the last time you enjoyed being loved while sober?

- Do you feel safe in intimate situations while sober?

- Do you often feel isolated from people, with a sense of loneliness?

- Do you often feel sad?

- Is anger something that you find hard to express?

- Do you find anger plays too big a role in your life?

All of the questions above are related to the different emotions of the Inner Child who lives in each and every one of us. Therefore, it is completely natural for us to experience all of these emotions at various times throughout our lives.

CHILDHOOD

The Inner Child is the child-like part of us that has never grown up, and is the part within us that should never grow up, for its sole purpose is to keep us in touch with our unprocessed emotions.

Some people have very few pleasant memories of their childhood. I do not know anyone who could say they had an unblemished and therefore perfect childhood. Most parents try to do their best for their offspring, yet often their ways of parenting may be about how they themselves were parented. Even their best intentions are at times perceived by the child as not what they want or need. Most children adore their parents and make the unconscious assumption that their parents must be right.

Every child interprets life differently within the family circle and it is this interpretation that is filed away in the software of the child's mind. The Inner Child of the unconscious mind desires only to receive love, warmth, safety and to have fun, just as you did in childhood. If you cannot recall these desires being met by your parents or family circle for whatever reason, then your Inner Child may have been suppressed earlier than normal.

BECOME MORE ADULT

If you had to grow up too soon – before you were ready – due to circumstances that were beyond your control, your adult part would have been created early in life to protect your Inner Child from being wounded. So you became more adult as a way to protect your feelings of fear and vulnerability and this was a natural protective reaction.

Your adult part is the part of you that now takes life too seriously, for it does not know how to laugh and enjoy life and it has a real problem with just being in the moment.

Often the adult part will not like chaos and will attempt a highly organised home and life. This keeps the adult personality safe until alcohol is consumed.

THE INNER CHILD AND ALCOHOL

The child within, when suppressed, will have the passionate desire to come out from hiding from time to time. The Inner Child loves both alcohol and food. It knows these are fun ways to achieve the sensations of the warm flow of feeling safe, calm and loved. These feelings can become the trigger to over-drinking in unhelpful ways. It may feel addictive or like an uncontrollable craving. The Inner Child can often be very demanding and will drive someone to drink too much on a regular basis.

As the Inner Critic becomes suppressed when we drink, the Inner Child comes out to play because it wants to have fun, experience passion and excitement. It wants to laugh!

Many men and women need to drink so that they can make love, give love or just have fun. They don't feel safe enough in the sober world to connect intimately.

The Inner Child loves alcohol, because alcohol is the key to the gate of the garden. The Inner Child might find itself allowed to tell a person that they are wonderful or to crack another joke. The Inner Child can't wait for you to have a few drinks, so its voice can be heard instead of the Inner Critic.

The Inner Child will seek out people who love to drink, a safe harbour. When sober, the adult man or woman may not be able to offer the love and warmth that the Inner Child can.

Allow yourself to imagine how much fun you could have with your Inner Child if you gave yourself permission to be that child, without a drink!

What if your brain and body felt safe enough to have a really good belly laugh while you were sober?

BEING INTIMATE

The Inner Child is the free-thinking, sexual and sensual part that exists within each and every one of us. The Inner Child loves being hugged, kissed and intimate. It is the part within us with passion and creativity that enjoys having sex. This is because it is an experience of being in the moment, of feeling safe and not alone.

Intimacy in a loving relationship is a wonderful experience, but how we achieve intimacy depends on our Inner Child's idea of how to get the intimacy it needs. It is a primitive part that doesn't think about the future or end result – all it wants is for its needs to be met right now.

Creating a safe haven for your Inner Child when sober will help to break the fear of intimacy and the need to drink to become a sexual person.

If you feel sober sex is an issue, my suggestion is to listen to the one of the Hypnosis Hub recordings and imagine, while sober, the sensation of skin on skin, lips on lips and the association of warmth, safety, love and respect.

Each week, while listening to the recordings, keep this brain training activity going. The more you experience the moments in your mind, the more your mind and body will become familiar and comfortable.

THE FEAR OF INTIMACY: MILES' STORY

Many people assume someone who has a lot of sex is confident in intimate situations; that is not always the case.

Miles came to see me about his regular heavy drinking. He had not had an alcohol-free day for over twenty years, which is much more common than people dare to discuss.

Miles had a typical bachelor lifestyle and the money that comes with it. His relationship history was characterised by short-term relationships and many one-night stands. I must admit Miles was very charismatic and I could see why the girls liked him.

When Miles told me 'I just had never found The One!' I knew his Inner Child was part of the problem.

Many people who have had a lot of sexual partners naturally assume this means they are good at sex, which can be true. They may not be good at the emotional side and will avoid connecting to their lover. They will defend their sexual life by suggesting they are looking for love when it is the complete opposite. They are, in fact, avoiding it by having a lot of sex as a smokescreen.

When Miles was twenty-one, he fell in love for the very first time. The relationship was short-lived as she broke it off to be with someone else. This devastated Miles. He said he still compares her to every girl he meets and none of them are good enough.

This is a common issue for people who have a fear of intimacy and Miles was no different. His mind had been traumatised by this break-up and he had decided to avoid getting close again in case he got hurt.

On one hand Miles craved love and intimacy, but equally he was in fear of it. So he drank alcohol as a way to console himself and to rid himself of his Inner Critic. This allowed his Inner Child to come out and play.

Miles couldn't tell me how many women he had slept with, but it was in the hundreds.

I asked him if he had ever had sober sex and he replied only when he was really hungover, and then he just wanted the girl to go away! 'I can't handle the conversations in the morning. They drive me crazy and then they want me to call them and it just gets too hard.'

Miles' self-esteem was affected from this early relationship trauma and this stirred his Inner Child that craved love, safety and warmth to come out. The problem was, alcohol had to be in his bloodstream first!

Miles was a very emotionally intelligent man and as we continued to talk he said to me, 'This isn't about drinking is it?' I replied. 'It's mainly about your heart and mind not moving on from this early relationship. You haven't healed. Alcohol has become a way to try and connect to this fun, loving and playful part of your personality to try and find it again. The challenge you have is your mind is searching for this love but only when you have been drinking. As you get older this isn't so much fun and it isn't so attractive to you and the women around you. It gets boring to do the same thing knowing you aren't getting anywhere. Which then can create more heavy drinking as the mind assumes this is the answer to the problem.'

Conflict can rage in our minds. One part wants to be loved while the other part thinks it is unsafe to be loved. In order to affirm that intimacy is a safe experience when sober, you need to embrace your Inner Child – without over-drinking.

What Miles and I focused on was training his mind to have sober conversations with women who had the integrity that he was looking for. I suggested starting off with women he knew already who were in a relationship or single. Either way it didn't matter. The goal was for his mind to become familiar, comfortable and confident in sober ways about spending time with women who had the qualities he sought in a partner.

Over a few weeks, Miles attempted this activity and he started to notice he was gaining sober social confidence. He said if he felt attracted to the woman involved he would retreat initially. The goal is to take small but strong steps.

ENJOYING LIFE SOBER

Being able to converse, have fun and enjoy life socially while sober supports your Inner Child to feel safe. Expecting the alcohol to bring this personality out can cause long-term intimacy issues. Being able to interact while sober does take practice but like all things in life worth doing, it takes time.

ALCOHOL MEANS THE INNER CHILD IS ALLOWED OUT TO PLAY

Alcohol is used by a lot of men and women as a way for their Inner Child to come out to play. When it becomes an emotional habit, down the track it can cause major problems with sex, fun and a spontaneity in life.

If we mistakenly believe drink is the only way to access the Inner Child, we lose the sense of the fun person we really are. We are also at risk of losing our personal credibility and self-respect too.

Thank goodness our Inner Child never goes away, and this is something we need to understand and continually work with. Our Inner Child state is the essence of who we are. Sadly, through life experiences, it can become suppressed and we feel that it has gone away and left us until we begin drinking: then, lo and behold, it releases itself and presents itself to the world. How often do we see people who are quite serious by nature become, after a few drinks, much lighter, softer and kinder? The more we practice releasing our Inner Child while sober, the more we will remember that feeling and start to own it.

EXPRESSING TEARS

As the Inner Critic is suppressed when we drink, some people may become tearful because they don't care much about the consequences until they wake the next morning and have a massive Inner Critic attack. The Inner Critic will say, 'You were such an idiot last night, what did you think you were doing? Everybody is going to laugh at you when you go into work on Monday. People are going to think you're screwed up because you couldn't stop crying.'.

The Inner Child sees drinking as way to express its sadness, abandonment issues and its fears about life, without the Inner Critic pointing the finger of blame. So often the drinker will feel embarrassed at the outpouring of tears and will avoid drinking just in case it may happen again.

SHUTTING DOWN THE INNER CHILD

The Inner Child doesn't know about responsibility – it only knows how to be. In the adult world, some of us mistakenly believe that being responsible as an adult means shutting down the Inner Child. Along the way, people close to us may have said things like: 'You're not a child any more' or 'You can't do that at your age'. To these people, adult behaviour means good work ethics, social standing and not rocking the boat. Who among us really wants to be serious and responsible twenty-four hours a day? No one!

A child who has experienced sexual, physical or emotional abuse will learn very quickly that remaining a child only exacerbates more abuse. Therefore, shutting down this innocent, wide-eyed, beautiful part of the self is the best method of protection. To these adults, being a child signals hurt and abandonment, so their Inner Child digs itself deep inside the unconscious mind. Why would you want to remain a child if this is what represents childhood memories?

In this situation alcohol could be the self-destruct button, and this could lead to alcohol dependency, drugs or worse. If you feel this is your situation and that you are suffering as a result of childhood abuse, seek out a reputable therapist to help heal your Inner Child.

SELF-EXPRESSION

Depending on your environmental upbringing, you may have experienced alcohol as either a way of celebrating good news or getting over stress, or it may have been used as an aid to help communication. If you came from a family where self-expression was difficult, then the chances are that you will use alcohol in adulthood as a way to free yourself to talk emotionally.

Women in general are relatively good at self-expression and some men appear to find self-expression more difficult. I believe it is because many of us have been brought up with the belief that men don't talk about intimate, emotional things, only women do. It is true that men find it more difficult to express their need for love because their Inner Child has been suppressed. Young boys, to this day, are still told: 'Big boys don't cry.' Of course this is a fallacy and only serves to create men who are scared to show their feelings.

I believe we all have the right to the sober self-expression in order to enjoy our life. For many people it takes practice to free the Inner Child and have fun without alcohol: it is an incredibly rewarding experience.

ANGER AND THE INNER CHILD

Anger is a major player when it comes to the suppression of the hurt and wounded Inner Child.

A wounded Inner Child can resort to alcohol, food or drugs and be attracted to abusive relationships simply because this is the only way the Inner Child knows how to be. It is sad but true: there are many wounded inner children walking around in adults, just waiting to express their anger, and this anger plays a major role in expressing the hurt and rejection that these adults felt during their childhood.

If when you drink you become angry, tearful and fearful, it is likely that your Inner Child does not know how to get and receive love. It never experienced love while you were growing up, and because of this it feels lost.

Not everyone has had a healthy childhood, and if alcohol brings out these negative emotions in you, please trust that the alcohol is demonstrating to you that you need to heal your Inner Child. Alcohol is not helping; rather, it is bringing up all the pain that you need to deal with. There are many therapists who are trained in Inner Child work.

While growing up, each of us has created emotional habits to enable us to cope and get on in life. Some adults learn to become aloof to protect themselves, or they become overly chatty because silences make them feel anxious and scared and remind them that they are in the moment. Habits develop as an emotional reflex action and this happened because we have, in childhood, limited knowledge of the world around us. Remember: food, love, tears and laughter are the first learned experiences in life. No wonder so many of us use alcohol as a way to nurture and bring forth our Inner Child.

THE WORD 'NO'

The Inner Child doesn't like the word 'no' or limitations, as this is an adult trait. So the more you drink, the more the child comes out as the Inner Critic suppresses itself.

The Inner Child within us all is open to new and exciting experiences. As we know, children get bored very easily. When a child is told 'no', the immediate reaction is to rebel or withdraw because the child does not have the capacity to comprehend all the rules and regulations of adult life. People who struggle with their drinking habit may also have this rebellious streak.

CREATIVITY: JACKIE'S STORY

One of most common reasons why people drink is to be creative. This is when the Inner Child comes out. This personality loves drawing, painting, writing and getting stuck into fantasy. In the sober life, creativity can be difficult to locate for many people.

Jackie, one of my clients, was in a difficult situation with her drinking. She had a full-time job but her real passion was writing. Jackie had recently written a TV drama script, which a friend in the television industry thought was really good. An agent got involved with the goal of approaching some producers.

The purpose of Jackie coming to see me was because, in the past, Jackie had written in the evenings once the kids had gone to bed. She worried that there was always a glass of wine or two consumed while she was writing. Jackie felt wine really helped her creativity. Nevertheless, now the agent had given her a deadline, she needed to write at other times of the day. This meant she needed to commit to spending weekends and, where possible, the early mornings to get the script finished.

Jackie attempted this routine but felt her writing wasn't as creative without wine in her bloodstream, which is when she decided to come to me to help with this issue.

I help a lot of writers become more trusting and creative, so I felt very comfortable helping Jackie with her dilemma.

I knew Jackie's creativity came from her Inner Child and with the help of wine it came out free-flowingly, while the Inner Critic was suppressed.

Together we worked on a plan to train her unconscious mind to go into the writing zone without the Inner Critic and wine in the equation. Jackie's mind learned how to calm herself down before she went into her writing space, so she was free to write with ease and the creativity flowed. This worked brilliantly and Jackie completed her script sober and felt really good about achieving something so important to her.

THE CONFIDENT, FUN INNER CHILD

How wonderful it is to see a child who is encouraged to embrace their childhood fully. There are three aspects of the confident child: the child that is allowed to be naughty while being safely cautioned and guided through their parents' unconditional love; the child who is encouraged to speak up and to be heard so that they can express an opinion; and the child who has the freedom to play and have wildly creative thoughts. I love to hear a child's delightful laughter and see the beauty in the smile on his or her face.

If you feel this was not part of your childhood, you can embrace these experiences as an adult. It is your right to be the version of you that you want to be! It does take practice but the lovely thing is your Inner Child is easily accessible. You can create new learning for yourself through your inner parent's eyes, not the parents you had or have but your own ideas of how you would like to parent your Inner Child – through doing this you can access and bring out your own confident, fun, child-like Inner Child while feeling safe.

Here is some 'play work' that can assist you to explore your own Inner Child safely, so you can enjoy spending more valued time with the innocent, fun-loving you:

Imagination

Find a few minutes to lie on your bed or sit in a chair, close your eyes and spend some time with your Inner Child. Do you have a clear image of yourself as a child? If not, look at a photograph or create an image in your mind that you feel best represents you as a child. Tell your Inner Child that you are always available as the inner parent no matter what happens, and that it is safe to be loved, to have fun and enjoy the wonders of life. This can be a highly emotional experience. No one will ever know your child the way you do. It is a very special relationship, a bond that will always be there. An Inner Child, when nurtured, will give you so much emotional support, laughter and lightness in your life.

SOMETHING TO THINK ABOUT ...

- Take a walk on your own to a place where you know you feel safe. Perhaps walk through a park, then take the time to sit and look at the beauty of nature. When we view nature through the eyes of the inquisitive child, we notice how much beauty there really is in this world. Notice the birds and the colours of the trees. If it is summer, explore the flowers, their perfume, the grass beneath your feet and the height and colour of the trees. If it is autumn, run through the fallen leaves, then have fun exploring, scatter them with your feet, scoop them into your hands then lift them high and let them fall. If it is snowing, make a snowman, snowballs or a snow angel. To do this lie on your back, arms spread out at shoulder height and wave your arms through the snow, then stand up and look at the beauty of the earth angel you truly are. If it is spring, notice how the buds are beginning to come out, enjoy exploring each flower and tree and notice how men, women and children smile as they enjoy the first signs of spring. Explore with your senses: touch, taste, smell, sight and hearing, for this is how a child explores and learns.

- Rent a really funny movie on your own or with someone you feel you can really be yourself with. Laugh like you want to laugh rather than suppressing it. Hire a movie that is a real tearjerker and have a fantastic cry all on your own. Laughing and crying are great ways of releasing the tensions, fears and anxieties of the Inner Child.

* Write a letter to yourself explaining that you did the best you possibly could as a child with the resources that you had at hand. Explain that as an adult you are going to make sure that you and your Inner Child can express to each other any emotions of fear, rejection, abandonment and love.

* Make a list of all the things you would love to do that you feel a little silly or shy about. An example could be joining an art or dancing class. Perhaps you could go to a pop concert that your adult part says you're too old for. You are never too old to enjoy life.

CHAPTER 6

THE EMOTIONAL SPECTRUM OF A DRINKER'S LIFE

Now that you understand the different inner personalities that drive people to drink, let's look at the different emotions that encourage unhelpful drinking too.

What I find fascinating about my work is how diverse drinkers are and the different reasons why they feel the need to drink more than they want to.

So, I am going to talk about an array of emotions that clients experience when it comes to drinking too much. You may resonate with some of their drinking situations and some of them you may not. Either way, what is important is for you to remember is that you are so much more than your drinking.

Emotions are feelings that can trigger unhelpful or helpful behaviour. People drink for many emotional reasons. The following are key.

ANGER: CHRISTOPHER'S STORY

Advocates of Chinese medicine believe that the liver stores anger. The emotion of anger can be so powerful and self-defeating. Many clients who want to drink less come to me with anger issues. Alcohol can calm someone down who is feeling angry; it can also trigger a volcanic eruption.

Christopher came to see me, after being referred by his wife. She was tired of his angry outbursts under the influence of alcohol. Their marriage was being tested as they had lost a lot of money in the financial crash in 2008 and had not been able to recover from it.

Christopher didn't say much about being angry when we met, but he did talk about the stress that money issues had created in their marriage. He worried how they could move forward in the current situation.

My heart went out to Christopher because he was like a lot of my clients where his pride at being the provider and the successful entrepreneur was being challenged.

Professional self-esteem is so important to many people and I find, with men in particular, that this is key to how they behave in their everyday life. If they've had a bad day at the office, this can adversely impact their partner or family.

Christopher was a quiet man who wasn't a good communicator. After ten minutes of conversation, I broached the Inner Critic aspect with him. He nodded and I felt he was now a little more comfortable with me. As discussed earlier, people drink to escape this voice. In Christopher's case, his upbringing, where big boys don't cry and don't express how they feel, inhibited him from being open when he was sober. His mind and body were feeling the pressure and couldn't wait for Christopher to drink to let all the anger out!

What was also an issue was Christopher's Perfectionist. As already mentioned, Perfectionists are bad losers and do not admit defeat well. Even though the financial situation had been triggered by a global crisis and was beyond his control, to a Perfectionist this is not acceptable.

Christopher and I worked on ways to release the anger in his everyday life before he drank. This meant his anger was being extinguished beforehand, so he would stop having alcohol-fuelled meltdowns in front of his wife.

BOREDOM

I can't tell you how often I hear the reason why people drink more than they want to is because they are bored!

Some people may see this as a lazy response to boredom. For a drinker, opening a fresh bottle of wine is instant entertainment.

A typical scenario of having a busy day at work, then coming home and feeling that there isn't much to do other than watch TV, is a common problem.

For those who have a rewarding career, boredom won't be an issue generally but it is a big issue for many drinkers, whether it spices up another evening or helps with that laborious phone call to your negative mother.

Drinking alcohol is a quick fix to boredom. When someone realises they are bored, if their mind has learned from the past that alcohol is the answer, then in a nano-second alcohol is deemed appropriate. This is even at 9.15 a.m. at your desk because you feel you have nothing exciting to do all day. It doesn't mean you will drink then, but it might set you up to look forward to having that drink in the evening.

Boredom can be make people feel anxious because it triggers the Inner Critic: 'You don't have enough things going on in your life!' or 'Why don't you start going to the gym or do something to stop this drinking in the evening?' The radio-crazy monologue of the Inner Critic can get so bad that drinking ends up being the quickest way to silence it. The party starts in the mind of a drinker as soon as the bottle is opened or the can of beer is poured. Then everything seems rosier.

For someone who is worried about their drinking

and feels their life is boring, it is important for them to find other ways of dealing with this, if it is an ongoing situation.

It's not just about training the mind and body to drink more slowly, but also about finding something else that stimulates sober self-esteem. It's about finding something that is entertaining without alcohol being in the equation.

It might sound a cliché but doing an evening course, whether online or at the local community centre, or deciding to do something that takes you out of your comfort zone, is good too. There are lots of ways to entertain yourself, but many of them require some effort.

If you are feeling bored with your life, make a list of all the things you want to do, whether you feel a little scared about attempting them or not. I always say a little bit of courage goes a long way. Do one thing differently or try something new. Put on one of the Hypnosis Hub recordings or one of the Hypno Blasts to get you motivated.

It is amazing how creative you can be when you are in an intuitive, relaxed state.

LONELINESS

Loneliness is a big issue for many people, whether single, widowed, someone who travels a lot for their work or a single parent. It is a very common reason why people drink more than they want to.

Boredom does come into play here too because someone spending a lot of time on their own can get bored of their own company. As for boredom, loneliness encourages the Inner Critic to voice itself. I often say to clients, 'Too much thinking time can be dangerous' and people who suffer from loneliness are all too aware of this problem. Too much thinking time, if in a bad space, can encourage depression and anxiety, which in turn can lead to drinking, and a lot of it!

There is no one to keep a solo drinker in check, so they don't care how much they drink. This is very common with parents when their children leave home. The empty nesters know their home drinking can be a problem but equally don't care because they've had their 'responsible' time as a parent. I think this is understandable. The problem is the home drinking can creep up and before the drinker knows it, they have finished their fourth gin and tonic and it's only 7 p.m.!

Single parents and people who live on their own can fall into the trap of drinking every night as a reward, and as a way of feeling better about being alone. A bottle of wine can seem like a friend. Perhaps you enjoy your own company, and you have a regular solo party to pat yourself on the back after a long day of childcare and working hard to pay the bills? Perhaps you lack the energy to create new kinds of entertainment. How about treating yourself to a boxset, or a film you've always wanted to watch?

LIZ'S STORY

Liz had been living alone for a long time. Loneliness was her biggest issue and it was causing her a lot of angst as she drank to deal with it. By the time she came to see me she was drinking two bottles of wine a night and three on the weekends. Liz's self-esteem was low and any motivation she once had had slowly deteriorated over the years.

She would spend whole weekends on her own where she wouldn't talk to anyone. She would get up in the morning, go out for a walk, do some shopping and then come home and open a bottle of wine at lunchtime because there was nothing else to do. Liz was depressed and felt no hope in her future, so she had lost the motivation to change her situation. Alcohol was holding her back.

The first thing we needed to focus on was getting her Intuitive Self to be more present in her life. I suggested she listen to one of her Hypnosis Hub recordings in the morning to start her day. It's a good time to listen to something positive then, so that the Inner Critic has less of a chance to get in there and sabotage the day before it starts! This was key to helping Liz get out of the habitual heavy drinking she had got herself into. It was strong, small steps for Liz, as her self-esteem started to reappear and she realised she didn't need to drink to enjoy her own company.

One of the most important things for Liz to learn was that being on her own can be a good thing. People who live alone have to be prepared to initiate phone calls and invite friends out. Those who live with others don't have to plan social activities as much and also don't have to leave their home to have physical interaction with another person.

Liz had lost her social self-esteem as the Inner Critic had suggested to her, 'No one will want to spend time with you so why bother inviting them?' Once Liz trained her mind and body to tune out the Inner Critic, she started to become more confident to connect with friends, and her social world started to improve. This difference alone gave Liz the space to enjoy being on her own, knowing there was a healthier balance between being home alone and out and about with friends.

Liz still drank at home, and sometimes more than she planned, but her drinking wasn't coming from a negative space any more, so her regular drinking was less.

PROCRASTINATION

Perfectionists, in particular, have an issue with procrastination. As they prefer to do only what they know they can achieve, they are unlikely to attempt the things their mind doesn't have positive references for. They often won't attempt things they feel they won't excel in because they don't want to come second and they don't want to appear to be a failure.

They often have to be under a lot of duress before they will achieve what they need to. Once they do start and complete something new, they feel really proud. Once their mind knows it is safe to do this, it will continue to confirm this behaviour as positive.

A Perfectionist student might cram all their studies into the last moment. Or a Perfectionist might finally tackle something that they truly don't want to do, like their tax return or clearing their cupboard out. Once they have started a new project, they will aim to excel at it because of their perfectionism.

Alcohol is a great way to procrastinate. Many people who drink alcohol will use drinking as an excuse to not do what they know they need to do. The longer the person puts off what needs to get done, the higher their anxiety, and so the cycle of drinking to avoid taking action continues.

HAVING FUN

The good news is, there is a wonderful emotion that encourages drinking which is being fun-loving. It's easy to blame the negative aspects of heavy drinking; sometimes people drink too much because they are caught up in the social aspect of life. They plan in advance before they go out in a positive way that they are going to have a hangover the next day.

Having fun and being in the moment is an important part of life. When you decide with some friends that you are going to have that extra bottle of wine because the night is going well and you all say 'Why not!', that is OK. Or when you decide that you are going to have that extra piece of homemade apple pie that has never tasted so good, or that champagne cocktail with your oldest and dearest friend.

As long as this doesn't become the cover-up to heavy drinking ways, socialising and having the odd hangover is acceptable.

HANGOVERS ARE OK

I never suggest to anybody who drinks that they will never have a hangover after working with me. In fact, I suggest the opposite. Life is not about measuring how many hangovers you do or don't have.

Professionally speaking, I don't have a problem with hangovers and I absolutely support having fun. But we shouldn't always need to drink to have fun, and if you do, then I suggest exploring your Inner Child. Perhaps it needs more opportunities when you are sober to enjoy the moment. How about climbing a tree, going beach-combing, collecting conkers, swimming in the rain?

It's about going with the flow of your life from a calmer, healthier perspective. When you do this, you know when the bell's ringing to tell you to stop drinking. This means you are not drinking to run away from your life or situations that are unhelpful to your self-esteem and emotional wellbeing, but to celebrate the moment.

I have a wonderful story to back this up, which I often tell to seminar participants.

CELEBRATE THE MOMENT: JONI'S STORY

A client of mine called Joni came to see me years ago about her drinking, and reduced successfully. She has since referred many new clients to me and remains an email buddy.

One day Joni told me a funny drinking story about a special night she had experienced recently.

'Georgia, my new boyfriend's best friend is a billionaire and he invited us to fly to New York from London on his private jet to spend the evening with him for his fortieth birthday. I was over-excited as he was paying for two nights in one of the swankiest hotels in New York, all expenses paid. He even gave us spending money so that we could buy whatever we wanted to wear to his birthday dinner on the Saturday night. So, here I am boarding a flight to New York with all these other people I didn't know, drinking expensive champagne. I couldn't help myself but have a bit more than I would normally drink. We arrived in New York pretty drunk and then went our own way that evening. The next day I bought a gorgeous dress, got ready for the birthday party, already planning to make the most of the evening by having lots of fun.

'The food was amazing and the wine ... we started with champagne, then white wine, then red wine, dessert wines, cognac and vintage ports. I asked the sommelier how much the average bottle of wine was that we were drinking. He said between $10,000 to $12,000 each! So, in one night, I had drank nearly two bottles of wine at the cost of US$22,000!'

I have hypnotised quite a few billionaires but I have never had the opportunity to drink with one, and I've never had the chance to consume such special wine.

There are times when drinking more than planned is fun or just happens because the people you are with, or where you are, feels right. In Joni's case, she was having a unique experience and part of that was sampling this incredible wine. And although she drunk a lot of alcohol that night, she made sure she had eaten as well. Joni knew it was about pacing and really tasting and savouring rather than gulping.

My focus is on the habitual, regular drinking that gets you into some tricky situations with yourself and the world around you. The fun drinking times we want to keep, because life is about having fun and being in the moment sometimes. We've all had great nights out when we've had too much to drink, felt under par the next day, but still had no regrets. Those were special nights.

I just love Joni's drinking story, and you may have some even better drinking stories to tell down the track.

Remember, drinking alcohol is not about being perfect but perfecting a balance. It's about drinking because you choose to, not because your mind says you have to in order to feel ok. This is the key difference you are learning to make about how you drink, when and why.

EXTERNAL CRITICS

One extremely important aspect of my work is to help clients deal with external critics. I touched on this earlier in the Radio-Crazy Syndrome chapter.

It's difficult enough having an Inner Critic, but the double whammy of having judgemental and critical people in your life can exacerbate the drinking problem.

External critics come in all shapes and sizes from parents, partners, children and even colleagues. I often refer to them as the alcohol police.

I spend a lot of time helping clients deal with external critics because it is key to their sense of self-worth. Nobody likes being judged, and when it comes from someone who is meant to love and care for you, it can cause a lot of vulnerability and emotional instability.

ISABELLA'S STORY

Isabella, single and in her mid-thirties, came to see me about her heavy drinking. Her story, sadly, is not unusual. She worked in a corporate environment where she was doing very well professionally. She was extremely articulate and charismatic with a wicked sense of humour.

Isabella came from a strict Jewish family. Every Friday night she would travel to her parents' house for the traditional Sabbath dinner. Her parents didn't know she drank alcohol and Isabella never wanted them to know. She felt it was her 'dirty little secret', which made her feel really guilty.

The same conversations would come up every Friday with her mother that made her feel awful about herself. Isabella's mother would ask, 'Have you met any nice Jewish boys this week?' and Isabella would roll her eyes and say, 'No Mum, I don't know any nice Jewish boys. I don't have time for a boyfriend. I work hard and I'm fine with this.' Isabella's mother would then continue with her ritual conversation: 'Nice Jewish boys don't like career girls. Isabella, you need to get married and have children like your brothers and your cousins. What's wrong with you? My friends look at me like I'm a bad mother and I feel you have failed me.'

Isabella said that this conversation was *every* Friday night. She felt guilty that she didn't enjoy spending time with her family because she felt like a failure.

So, around 8 p.m., Isabella would leave her parents' home and drive to her apartment where she would drink two bottles of wine. She said she would literally drink herself to sleep with the guilt of not giving her parents what was expected of her. Her mother confirmed what her Inner Critic said, that she was a failure. Not only did Isabella have the issue of the stress of her inner negative world and the impact it had on her, but her outer world confirmed there was something wrong with her.

Isabella told me that her failure to live up to her mother's expectations drove her to work harder professionally. She felt romantically there was something wrong with her and so she would never attempt nor contemplate a meaningful relationship, because she felt that men wouldn't like her.

I say this often to single clients: sometimes it takes more courage to be single than to be in a relationship. Isabella hadn't met anyone she connected with which is absolutely acceptable. As I said to her, 'Why settle for a relationship that is not good for you?' I believe it is better to be on your own than in an unhealthy relationship.

PARENTS' SELF-ESTEEM

Many parents' self-esteem comes from their children, and Isabella's mother had a powerful Inner Critic of her own. It told her she had failed as a parent and she was an embarrassment to her family and friends.

It's a common problem when a parent's desire for a child to be a doctor or a lawyer is because they didn't have the same opportunities as their child. They have a mistaken belief that what is right for them must be right for their children.

Like Isabella, many children who grow up with critical parents have very low self-esteem and often high levels of anxiety. This is because the child's Inner Critic becomes their strongest voice and they lose sight of any true potential they have in another direction. Often, the children of critical parents, or parents who expect their child to be perfect, will fulfil their desire and become a lawyer or a doctor just to please their parents. Such a person can have an effective combination of the Pleaser and the Perfectionist personalities. They learn what they need to do in order to receive the most amount of love from their family to please them, even to the detriment of what truly makes themselves happy. The Perfectionist keeps them in check to make sure they achieve their goals.

A child who grows up with critical parents can develop strong addictive behaviours as a way to suppress inner and outer fears about not being good enough. This is when alcohol can become an issue.

WORKPLACE BULLYING

External critics are abundant in the workplace. Many corporate clients came to see me in my London clinic with massive drinking issues due to workplace bullying.

Having to deal with being in an environment where your boss or fellow workers belittle you can be beyond stressful, as there is nowhere to hide. I love the saying, 'What other people think of me is none of my business' but it is difficult to accept this when you are worrying you are doing something wrong the whole time.

It's easy to assume there is something wrong with you, but it is the bully at work who has the problem. Critical and judgemental people are drowning in low self-esteem. They cover it up by making sure other people feel worse than they do.

I know many clients who were once very confident professionally, but because of a bad workspace experience, started to drink excessively. They feel so trapped in their work life and use alcohol as a form of escape.

Being assertive is key, and the Hypnosis Hub section will help you to deal with critical and judgmental people on a regular basis to stay strong and true to yourself around these people.

These people don't like it when a belittled person becomes strong but hey, so what! Bring it on!

THE DISOWNED SELVES: EMMA'S STORY

The disowned selves are the personality traits that we are not generally conscious of. They are suppressed in our everyday life because the Inner Critic believes they will harm us emotionally.

Disowned selves are created when we recognise that parts of our personality are not welcome in our family. It could be that, as a teenager, your mother told you that good girls don't have sex till they are engaged and the sexual part of you became suppressed. Maybe your sister was good at maths and you didn't want to compete with her, so to please her you hid your ability to keep the family system more cohesive. Disowned selves are created mainly in childhood but can be created later in life too.

As mentioned before, one of the key aspects of the Inner Critic is to make sure we are safe in the world we live in. The disowned selves can't wait for us to have a few drinks, as they are rejected in our sober life.

When we drink alcohol, the disowned personalities come out to play because the Inner Critic has gone away.

Emma, a client of mine, once felt dread going out because she knew when she drank too much she became really loud and sometimes obnoxious. Historically, her behaviour had got her into some trouble and friends had pulled her up on her aggressive behaviour.

In Emma's sober life, her Inner Critic restricted her communication to the outside world by suggesting that she would be rejected if she spoke the truth. Unbeknown to her, Emma felt angry that others had a voice while she didn't. Emma was chomping at the bit to have her say and engineered opportunities to drink so that she could express issues she felt she couldn't discuss without alcohol.

Perhaps her parents had once said she wasn't smart enough or once upon a time she was vilified in public for being incorrect about something. Whatever had happened in the past, Emma had learned to hold herself back when she was sober with people around her.

Emma needed to learn that she didn't need to drink to express what she really wanted to say.

If you drink to express an aspect of your personality trait that needs a sober voice, listen to the Hypnosis Hub recordings. They will help you to become more comfortable with who you are in the sober world, so you don't need to drink to bring out this part of your personality.

THE AUTHENTIC SELF: TERRY'S STORY

Another client called Terry grew up in a home where being a boy meant being a sporty person. His father demanded that he participate in all the traditional football matches, tennis and swimming. As a child he accepted that this was what he had to do, because he wanted the love from his father. As discussed in the Inner Child chapter, all children want to be loved and accepted and will go to great lengths to do this. What a child is really passionate about that is not acceptable to a parent, can be to the detriment of building a healthy sense of self. This means self-esteem is affected and the child grows up feeling that who they really are is not good enough. So they abandon their true self in favour of what gives them the support.

What Terry instinctively loved was dancing. As a child his father told him dancing was for girls and that no son of his would be a dancer because 'all dancers are gay.'

When Terry was in his twenties he discovered alcohol in a big way. He loved his beers and discovered that after a few of them he was a really good dancer. One day, after a few beers, he started watching a dance competition on television and couldn't keep his eyes off the screen and decided to record the whole series so that he didn't miss out.

The next morning he was horrified that his drunken self wanted to watch this show but had a strong feeling he shouldn't delete the series link.

Terry, like many people, drink alcohol as a way to bring forward the true person within. I call it the 'authentic self'.

RETRAIN YOUR MIND

I often ask clients who are unhappy with their professional life, 'What would you like to do if you didn't have to be a nurse or a teacher?' So often I hear, 'Georgia, I would like to be a writer or become an entrepreneur because I have some ideas but it all is a bit silly really.' I ask them when they feel this aspiration to be a writer or start that new business? More often than not, it is after they have had a few drinks.

The budding writer within often comes out when someone has had a few beers or wines and they start to surf the internet for writing courses or sit down at their laptop and draft a few ideas. Then in the morning they are shunted by the Inner Critic suggesting, 'That was a load of crap' and the inspired-while-drinking person is moved into the background until the next drinking stint.

Disowned selves are key to understanding who you are authentically and what passions you truly have in life. Alcohol can bring these traits to the forefront for many; however, there is another way.

Finding who you are authentically and embracing who you are in your sober life is so important. It means you can be who you truly are and when this feels comfortable, it means you don't need to drink to locate, create and accommodate this part of you.

The other day I was sitting on a train as a group of women were cursing some teenagers for laughing about their new teacher, a Mrs Littlebottom, because she had a rather large rear end. My question for those uptight, sober women would have been, would you have been laughing along if you had had a few wines under your belt? Probably yes. We often drink to express our child-like traits of fun and exploration.

If you feel you are too serious while sober and drink as a way to have fun, then now is the time to train your mind to feel safe to be authentic while sober. It's time to write, dance, laugh, create, speak up or be more confident sexually, without alcohol in your bloodstream.

CAN YOU FIND YOUR DISOWNED SELVES?

It is easy to find your disowned selves, simply by recognising how you behave when you are sober and after you have had a few drinks. How often have you discovered that you go out with a serious person and after a few drinks they turn out to be quite funny or interesting?

Primary Self (sober)	Disowned Self (after a few drinks)
Orderly	Disorderly
Relaxed with people	Suspicious of others' motives
Kind	Judgemental
Diplomatic	Truthful
Cold	Caring
Boring	Interesting
Unconfident	Gregarious
Sexually repressed	Confident sexually and/or promiscuous
By the book	Risk-taker
Unimaginative	Creative
Adult	Child
Pleaser	Assertive
Perfectionist	Don't care what others think

The goal is to incorporate these disowned selves so that they are present when you are sober as well.

YOUR RELATIONSHIP WITH OTHERS: PATRICIA'S STORY

As a child we are in a micro world, so we can safely avoid our disowned selves; when we go out into the big adult world, we meet people who represent those disowned selves. We tend to be most critical of those people whose traits we have repressed in ourselves. This can stir a lot of vulnerabilities as we cuss them and criticise them for their behaviour. Deep down we fear we too have these parts within us, because we actually do!

Patricia worked with an aggressive boss who always lashed out verbally at her. She was too scared of him to even resign and lived in a world of fear, insomnia and excessive drinking, to cope with her anxiety about her work.

Patricia's boss was a reflection of her disowned self. I am not suggesting that Patricia needed to be aggressive and lash out to hurt people, but if she had brought a little of that energy forward she could have been assertive with her boss. He, in turn, wouldn't have treated her that way because she would not have let him get away with it. Instead she drank that bottle of merlot every night and was aggressive with her partner who just couldn't understand why he took it out on her.

PEOPLE WE ADMIRE

Another way to find out who represents our disowned self is to find someone who we admire. The personality traits, or professionally what they do, trigger a strong desire to be that person. In the sober world, the Inner Critic will suggest this person is out of our reach, whereas this could not be further from the truth.

Anybody can climb mountains when they have tenacity, mixed with courage and an unwavering faith. It does take practice but trust me, anything is possible.

So, if you know there is someone whom you aspire to be like, or even someone you secretly envy, remember you can be that person with some practice. The next chapter will show you how to do this, so keep reading!

GOOD COMMUNICATION

Remember, people only get away with bad behaviour because we allow it. Our disowned selves live around every corner, in homes and most offices.

Through training your mind to value a little bit more of your disowned self, you will learn to own and value that personality, which means that you will have a healthier communication with the world you live in. You won't be grabbing for that drink because you will know that you would rather experience and express your true self sober. So you won't need to drink to be who you are authentically.

SOMETHING TO THINK ABOUT ...

- Keep a diary noting all the emotions you feel every day. Monitor which ones drive you to drink.

- While you are drinking, jot down any inspiring thoughts you have or things you like to do, which may lead to your disowned selves.

- Notice any unhelpful emotions you experience while you are drinking. This is key to locating a disowned self that needs to be expressed in your sober life.

- Start to exercise your disowned selves in sober moments in the privacy of your own time, so they can start to feel comfortable.

CHAPTER 7

YOUR PRESENT AND YOUR FUTURE

I have explained the science of your mind and its relationship to alcohol consumption. Now we are going to take it to a deeper and much more profound level.

Once a client has understood which parts drive them to drink, we can focus on moving forward. There are two key aspects of my work that need to take place in order for someone to drink less in their present and in their future.

CREATING NEW PRESENT MOMENTS

Every moment of your life, you have reacted in a particular way because of your history. In particular, your drinking history has determined your everyday relationship with alcohol.

So it is no surprise when someone says to me, 'Georgia, I just can't seem to drink less. The plans I make in the morning to not drink that evening go out the window by 5 p.m. when I am sculling my first vodka and tonic. What is my problem?'

I hear this conversation so regularly with clients. The habitual over-drinking, accompanied by regular anguish, annoyance and fear about their drinking can exacerbate the problem. This is not because they are a hopeless case, but rather because the Inner Critic fuels self-doubt from their history. It cannot find any evidence of success of drinking less alcohol. You need to create evidence of success, so your mind can use these new references as your truth and habit.

If your conscious mind and your unconscious mind have different opinions, the unconscious mind will always win!

I'll say it in another way. If you decide on a Monday that you are going to drink less this week and you don't drink less, it isn't because you are weak-willed at all. Your mind genuinely thinks that drinking the way you currently do is normal and effective as it blocks difficult feelings, thus helping you to avoid vulnerable moments.

Until you communicate with the deeper part of your mind that trained this unhelpful drinking behaviour to become a habit, it will continue. Frustratingly, worrying about it may make it worse. The more you think about the drinking issue, the more anxious you become. It's a bit like asking you not to think about an elephant with pink spots!

I believe that if someone wants to reduce their alcohol consumption, the easiest and most simple way is to use hypnosis.

EXERCISING YOUR MIND

Let's say if you decide you are going to participate in a half marathon this year, you would plan how to do this. You would gradually expose yourself to longer distances, so your body became more used to being fitter and stronger. You would not expect yourself to just go out there ill-prepared because your mind knows the chances of success would be minimal.

The same rule applies to your mind about alcohol. If you expect that tomorrow you will just drink two glasses of wine when your brain and body are used to drinking two bottles of wine, it will need some practice. Your mind needs exercise to prepare for this new activity, so that it becomes familiar and comfortable.

Your mind needs the exercises that come within the Hypnosis Hub recordings, to become familiar with the emotional and physical adjustments you are making.

DON'T RUN BEFORE YOU WALK

So many clients feel they have let themselves down because their Perfectionist says they must only drink three beers over three hours, and they feel like a failure because they didn't do the drinking perfectly. But no one is perfect, including you!

Don't try and run before you walk. The Hypnosis Hub recordings will help you create new drinking references that will become stronger, deeper, bolder and more comfortable with each drinking experience.

IMAGINATION IS IMPORTANT

One tool I just love is learning how to be in the present.

- Find somewhere to sit quietly, in your own space. Close your eyes and let your mind drift to past, pleasant memories. Find situations and scenarios that induce a sense of calm and feeling safe. Welcome any imagery that comes with it, such as a warm, sunny day at the beach or smelling the country air on a crisp, cold morning. It could be a lovely Sunday afternoon having a roast dinner with your family. Whatever the scenes are, they should invite a sense of wellbeing and safety.

- Now stay in this space as much as you can. Then imagine yourself drinking cool, clear water – maybe with a slice of lime and some ice. Keep imagining these scenes of safety matched with the fresh taste of water being consumed.

- Make a commitment to yourself that each time you think about drinking at times when you know it is not appropriate to drink, bring in thoughts and feelings that make you feel safe, then imagine drinking water.

This exercise will help to break the state of thinking about drinking at inappropriate times. It is a quick way to bring yourself into a good space.

Imagination is so important, as without it your mind will continue to bring up old memories that reflect unhelpful drinking days and ways.

Many clients say to me that their imagination is poor, but I can assure you this is not true. I respect that some people's imagination is more auditory or kinaesthetic, such as hearing the sounds of birds or feeling the breeze on their skin. Imagination is not just seeing, it is feeling, tasting, breathing and more. Each person's imagination will be different with the balances of the senses. Whatever works for you is right for you.

BEING IN THE PRESENT WHEN DRINKING

The more you rehearse this simple imagery exercise, the more your unconscious mind will take this on board as a real experience. This technique is a light hypnotic state that you can dip in and out of even when you are about to dive into that drinking session.

If you are feeling anxious and know you are about to drink with someone who is a heavy drinker or someone who makes you feel socially anxious, nip to the toilet and do the above exercise. Or you can listen to the Hypno Blast related to socialising so you can feel safe to drink less while out with people.

Being in the present moment and trusting in your ability to drink less takes practice. This exercise, along with the Hypnosis Hub recordings, will help you to achieve this.

It's the emotions *before* you drink that are important. If you are anxious, you are more likely to drink quickly. If you practice this exercise and/or the Hypno Blasts regularly before your first drink, your mind is well on its way to encouraging you to hydrate with water, drinking more slowly and drinking less.

So the next time you feel a sense of anxiety about your drinking, know it is your Inner Critic just playing games with you. Remember, the Inner Critic is working on your history of drinking. It only knows what it knows. It is up to you to change the record and you can do it by working on this one technique and listening to the Hypnosis Hub recordings.

This will help your mind and body to recognise that each drinking experience is separate from the next. Your mind will continue to build new references that support drinking in healthier ways. If you occasionally drink too much, the mind will know this is not your normal style of drinking.

You can do this!

MAKE IT A NEW HABIT

Drinking in healthy ways needs to become familiar. Your mind only knows what you give it and until you change this pattern of thought before you drink, it will continue to drink in ways that make you feel bad about yourself.

Your mind and body need to become familiar with this change in your drinking behaviour, so that healthy drinking becomes a habit. Habits are so familiar and comfortable that we do not question them. A habit is defined as: 'A settled or regular tendency or practice, especially one that is hard to give up' (oxforddictionaries.com).

Hard to give up! Wow. Wouldn't it be amazing if your regular habitual drinking was slow, healthy and moderate and hard to give up? The Hypnosis Hub recordings will seek to your brain so you are a calm, well-paced and emotionally balanced drinker.

HYPNOSIS HUB RECORDINGS IN YOUR EVERYDAY LIFE

How often do you think, 'I've had a busy day looking after everybody else. Now I am going to pour myself a big glass of wine/beer/brandy' or whatever?

Now, what I would like you to do is pour yourself some time instead. Just a small window of twenty-five minutes to start to make a commitment to yourself to do something good for you.

Being in the present can be difficult for some people, in particular if you have a strong Perfectionist personality. I can assure you that taking time out of your busy and demanding day by listening to just one of the Hypnosis Hub recordings will do so much for you.

The Hypnosis Hub is your time to recharge your emotional batteries, so you function in healthier ways. This time is about learning to be more in the present. When people are in the present they are not worried about the past or the future. Being in the present allows your mind and body to have some time out. Being in the present means that nothing is more important, and this is seriously good for your emotional wellbeing.

Make a pact with yourself that you will do something good for you. Remember, the more you practice and make a habit of listening to the Hypnosis Hub recordings, the more your mind and body will become familiar with this time. It's not just about you learning to drink less, but equally how you respond to your emotional life and the world around you.

Taking just twenty-five minutes out of your day or, at least using one of the short Hypno Blasts, will help you train your brain and body to cope better with life, so you don't need to drink too much as a coping strategy.

It is a gift to yourself to do this. I can't emphasis this enough. So my question to you again is, 'Who looks after you?' You are learning to look after yourself in much healthier and supportive ways by listening to the Hypnosis Hub recordings.

CONFIDENTIALITY IS IMPORTANT: KEN'S STORY

Ken was a typical client who told me he had absolutely no time for the recordings and also he didn't want his wife to know about him coming to see me. As I explained to him, if he wanted success he needed to find the time somehow, somewhere. I appreciated the confidentiality aspect was extremely important to him as his wife was his external critic.

A lot of people don't want their partners or family members to know they are worried about their drinking, which is absolutely fine. In many cases I encourage clients not to disclose their drinking fears to others because, once again, it encourages the Inner Critic to be more vocal. The Inner Critic loves someone being found out and exposed. The Inner Critic tells the drinker that now someone else knows, they will be watching and this can cause undue anxiety at a time when they need to feel as confident as possible.

It is nobody else's business but yours when it comes to why and how you drink. My goal is to give you tools and resources so you can belong to a drinking world that sees you drinking in positive ways.

Ken and I agreed that he would tell his wife his work had started meditation classes at lunchtime. It was an acceptable little white lie (we touched on this earlier). At first his wife seemed shocked as it was out of character but it actually made her warmer towards him. She knew how much meditation had helped so many of her friends.

Little white lies can be helpful sometimes when you want to keep yourself protected, so you can achieve your goal. Of course, down the track, if you want to tell someone who truly cares for you the truth, please tell them.

EVIDENCE IS KEY: WILL'S STORY

One of my clients, Will, was doing really well. His mind had generated good references of his drinking alcohol in healthy ways and he felt on top of his drinking. I was so pleased for him because he had been a classic Perfectionist drinker.

Some time later he emailed me to say that he had slipped back into his old drinking patterns. I was surprised but equally I knew something had been triggered, so we agreed another appointment was necessary.

Will's story was all too familiar: 'I was doing so well and then all of a sudden I had this big night out with the boys. I don't know what got into me but I just drank way too much. I woke in the morning feeling just awful. I felt like I had gone back to my old ways of drinking and I was really annoyed with myself!'

> Will is typical of many drinkers who have one blip and their Inner Critic suggests they have fallen off the wagon, thus they have failed. However, this was not true. Will's mind had copious amounts of evidence of success at drinking in a paced way.
>
> This is exactly the moment when Will should have started back with his recordings.

MIND MAINTENANCE

Your brain needs exercise too. After a few weeks you can slow down on your daily Hypnosis Hub recordings if you choose, but I recommend keeping a mind maintenance programme going.

Instead of every day or every other day, you listen to one of the recordings a few times a week. There are so many important messages in the recordings that will help you to live a better life all round. The Hypnosis Hub moments are about stabilising your emotions, connecting to the feelings of being safe and trusting in the moment, whether it is time to drink alcohol or not.

When I am feeling wobbly about something, the first thing I ask myself is, 'What is my Inner Critic suggesting?' and 'What am I scared or anxious about?' It's this exact moment that I know I need to go into my own space and process these fears. To have a healthy conversation with my Inner Critic and destabilise its energy with the truth, not what it thinks will happen!

Writing down what the Inner Critic says is a very helpful tool. It will give you great insight into its ongoing fears about you and your life. I am often so surprised to hear what my Inner Critic thinks is going to happen. Writing down its voice can be liberating and often laughable. What it thinks is going to happen in reality is often not even possible.

Keep an emotional diary of what feelings come up at any given time in the day. Monitor these emotions, so you can gauge how much they are affecting your life. So many emotions are built on old, out-of-date habits that do not reflect who you are now. Being in the present, once mastered, can give you an enormous amount of energy and confidence to enjoy being in the now. When you are in the now moment, there aren't the worries and unrealistic expectations people often place on themselves. Drinking less is more about what emotional space you are in before you start to drink. Learning to be in the present is instrumental to a healthy drinking habit.

THE CRYSTAL-BALL SYNDROME

One of the Inner Critic's claims to fame is that it tells you it can see into your future. It pretends to be your own personal psychic and if you believe it to be true you can get yourself into some bad drinking ways very easily.

As discussed, our anxieties and fears are partly driven by the amygdala. One of its main goals is to keep us on high alert, just in case something bad might happen. This part of the brain doesn't know if what it predicts will happen, but it will keep us on our toes, just in case it does.

The Inner Critic is the voice of the amygdala. It is the inner voice that will pretend it knows your drinking future, even though it has no evidence of it.

What I love about discovering the truth about the Inner Critic is that it has no resources whatsoever to see into your future. It never could and it never will be able to. It is working purely from the history of your drinking as the evidence of your future drinking. It truly believes that if it gets in first with some suggestions that you might drink too much, then you won't. The fear and anxiety it creates drives us to drink, even when we don't want to.

YOUR DRINKING FUTURE

Can you imagine having a mind that looks into your future without the Inner Critic there?

Can you imagine having a mind that can create future drinking habits that is supported by the Healthy Confident You?

This is what we are going to focus on with the last Hypnosis Hub recording. Whether you have time to listen to the twenty-five-minute recordings or have just five minutes before you go out to listen to the Hypno Blast social recording, get into the habit of self-caring in a positive way by taking some time out with these recordings.

One of my favourite hypnosis moments is when I help clients train their mind and body to look ahead into their own future. It's a powerful tool that I use a lot myself before I speak in public, or when I need to look into the future with more hope and faith.

CELEBRITIES LOVE THIS TECHNIQUE

You may not be aware that many famous sportspeople and well-known performers in the entertainment industries from around the world use this specific hypnotic technique with amazing results.

Clients come and see me about whatever their issues may be and they then request that I help them improve their golf or their tennis, for example. You would be surprised what else you can accomplish by simply listening to the Hypnosis Hub recordings that have nothing to do with drinking. There is so much scope to improve other areas of your life too.

I am now going to share with you one of the most effective hypnotic techniques with the aim of you becoming an expert yourself in this method. It doesn't take much. So any unhelpful Inner Critic suggestions – just let them go!

WILL THE HEALTHY DRINKING HABIT LAST?

When someone comes to see me, they generally bounce into my clinic after the first appointment feeling really empowered by their drinking week. They often say to me, 'It feels too good to be true. I am feeling so great about how much less I am drinking. I am worried my drink less habit won't last!'

This is a very common concern, which can undermine the best-laid plans. This is the Inner Critic suggesting that it won't last. The good news is that it can. I will explain how to use the recordings to get the best results.

THE MIND'S EYE TECHNIQUE

When a client comes to see me for their second appointment, I always use what I call the Mind's Eye Technique. It is an instant boost and a big kick up the bottom for the Inner Critic!

This is a brilliant tool that I use with people from all walks of life, whether they come to see me to drink less, have a fear of flying or want to stop smoking.

In order for any client to achieve the ultimate success, this technique needs to be there. Without it, long-term success will be limited.

The Mind's Eye Technique is all about visualising drinking events before they happen. Perhaps you have a special social event lined up where you know you are going to be drinking, or you've had an unusually stressful day and you know you want to drink that gin and tonic when you get in the door. Maybe you have a night out with friends, big personalities who are likely to dominate the conversation.

- First, put the second twenty-five minute Hypnosis Hub recording on or if you don't have that much time, the five minute Hypno Blast Social recording.

- Imagine feeling calm and safe before you drink, while you are drinking and picture yourself say 'no' when the bell rings so that you know when to stop drinking.

- Imagine yourself waking up in the morning remembering conversations from the night before, seeing wine left in the fridge door and that last sneaky drink still in the whisky bottle.

- Feel pride and self-confidence as your mind marries these positive emotions with drinking less.

The more you practice social and emotional moments in your mind before you get there, the more your mind will enact them in reality.

CHALLENGING MOMENTS

The Mind's Eye Technique is a wonderful tool to help set the scene about how you are going to handle your future before you get there. If, for any reason, it doesn't go to plan, it is important to trust that something better is around the corner.

There is this lovely story about a man in a small village who owned a very old car that he used as a taxi. One day the car stopped in the middle of the road and wouldn't start. To his despair the local garage told the old man it would be too expensive to replace. The man was very sad and worried because this was his livelihood and he knew it wouldn't be long before he would be unable to pay his rent.

Out of desperation he went to the church in the centre of town and for the first time in his life he prayed. He asked if God could send him a car, nothing fancy, and that a second-hand car would suffice his needs. Weeks went by without anything happening and the man was getting a little annoyed with God.

Then one day there was a knock at the man's door and lo and behold there was a fifteen-year-old Ford sitting there. The car had been left to a lady down the road who didn't want it, as she didn't drive, so she gave it to the man knowing he needed one. The man was ecstatic and told her how grateful he was. Later that day the man went to the church in the middle of town and thanked God for his second-hand car.

To the man's surprise God spoke to him and said, 'I'm pleased you are happy with your car; however, I had a Rolls Royce waiting for you!'

A RANGE OF DIFFERENT OUTCOMES

Sometimes what we plan in our minds is less than we truly deserve. This is because of low self-worth or past experience – perhaps the mind doesn't have enough evidence of life changing in more positive ways. Remember, there is a range of possible outcomes in any situation. The mind works on memories so when someone plans an outcome that they believe will happen and it doesn't happen, that is OK. I believe there is often a grander picture out there waiting for us. As people often say, when you least expect it life can change for the better.

I have so many wonderful stories from clients about what happens when clients use the Mind's Eye Technique. I would like to share one story in order to invite you into a world where things are more possible than you think right now.

EMERGENCY MIND MAKEOVER: GRACE'S STORY

Grace was unhappily single. She had tried Internet dating, local community courses, blind dates with friends of friends and more. By the time Grace came to see me she was really depressed and felt there was no hope of meeting a man.

She spent many nights at home drinking on her own which encouraged her Inner Critic to suggest many unhelpful scenarios about her future.

Prior to Grace coming to see me, she met with a hypnotherapist who told her that drinking on her own was a sign that she had a drinking problem. This therapist ushered her out of the appointment forbidding her to drink at home, which caused her to panic about her drinking.

I know people who live on their own who enjoy their solo drinking time, and Grace was no different. She didn't want to go out every night in order to drink, and felt very anxious about being told she had a drink issue.

By the time Grace came to see me she was in a bad way. Her Inner Critic was giving her such a hard time about her home-alone drinking that it made her drink even more! This led to more anxiety and self-esteem issues.

I was horrified that her therapist had told Grace that drinking on her own was a sign of alcoholism. This therapist had suggested she stop drinking, when it was not the drinking that was the problem. It was her thinking that was the problem!

It is unfair for people who live on their own or are single who are bullied into thinking there is something wrong with them for drinking at home alone. It's difficult to meet someone and even more challenging to meet the person who is truly good for you.

One of the first things that Grace and I worked on was using the Mind's Eye Technique to re-imagine her future. I couldn't bear any longer seeing such a gorgeous woman in such a horrible state.

One of the aspects of Grace's life we worked on hypnotically was to imagine her being with someone who had the qualities she admired in a man. We worked on magnetising this male energy into her life without the physical image of him. It was just about the energy and integrity of this man because I didn't want Grace's mind to set too much in stone.

Some weeks later her cousin died of terminal cancer. She attended the funeral and at the wake in the late afternoon she started talking to a man called Sean. They are now married. Grace's whole perspective on her life and her expectations had shifted as a result of the work we did together.

If you feel you deserve a bright future and you can visualise it, then it is more likely to happen. It is all about refocusing on the Happy Confident You, so that your Inner Critic isn't such a powerful voice. This is such an important tool to use so you can plan in advance how you want to respond.

CREATING A POSITIVE OUTCOME

Sometimes, out of awful situations amazing things can happen. A mixture of trust, a sense of faith and a good dose of the Mind's Eye Technique will help you guide yourself into a more positive future.

When you are in a state where you just don't know how the problem is ever going to resolve itself, rest assured that it will eventually resolve itself, often in ways you couldn't have imagined.

So, as a lovely exercise whenever you feel you can't see the situation improving or changing, use the Mind's Eye technique to get you into a better space, to help you to trust in your unknown future so much more.

THE MIND'S EYE TECHNIQUE FOR LIFE

- Go beyond the event or situation you are concerned about and visualise yourself feeling free and happy.

- Don't try and find the answers as to how it will be resolved, just try to trust and let go. There is a bigger picture that you can't see right now.

- Use the Hypnosis Hub recordings to imagine any future drinking event, waking without a hangover and feeling good about you.

SOMETHING TO THINK ABOUT ...

- You have an amazing mind. By using the Hypnosis Hub recordings you will be training your brain and body to feel better before you drink, so that you don't need to drink to feel calmer or safer.

- The recordings will help you to drink from a space of calm and wisdom. This is your gift from you to you.

- It takes practice but with a little bit of patience and a little bit of time out with the recordings, you will be drinking less naturally and easily.

Enjoy!

Warm regards,
Georgia
www.georgiafoster.com

HOW TO USE THE RECORDINGS

There are two Hypnosis Hub recordings and two shorter Hypno Blast recordings included with this book.

All you have to do is to sign up via this link at: www.georgiafoster.com/hypnosishub

The website link will ask you to fill in your name and email. You will then receive in your inbox login details including your own unique password (please check your spam folder).

Use the recordings as suggested below. You may choose to use the Mind's Eye Technique when you want to feel positive about your future. While listening, remember, if you have a strong Inner Critic it may not want you to imagine good things happening to you in the beginning, and that is fine.

This is typical of someone who has high levels of anxiety, so don't attempt, just listen. I will be guiding your mind to drink less even when the Inner Critic may suggest otherwise.

Listen as much as you can and know that if you fall asleep or have a busy brain the good news is that you are experiencing hypnosis. Drinking less is becoming more your reality. Please just trust.

Listen to **the first twenty-five minute recording** after chapter 2, as it covers the mind and body tuning into the prefrontal cortex before you drink. Also included in this recording is a section about training your mind and body to tune out of the Inner Critic and to connect to the authentic you, the Healthy Confident You.

Top tip: use this recording when you are having an Inner Critic moment or when you have had a challenging time and need to rebalance yourself emotionally, so that you are in a better space before you have your first drink.

The second twenty-five minute recording deals with your Pleaser, Perfectionist and Inner Child so you can enjoy these parts of your personality without feeling scared to say no to people or trying to be perfect. This recording is about having more fun when sober too! Also included is the Mind's Eye Technique, so that you can start to rehearse looking into your future with more wisdom and trust while feeling calm.

Top tip: use this recording when you need to make decisions, are feeling a little scared about your future or just generally need to feel better about the journey of your life.

The **Hypno Blast 1** is for your home drinking moments. You need to be stationary so that you can listen without being disturbed. This recording is a brilliant tool to put on before your drinking at home begins. It is a confidence booster, which can be used after a challenging day when you know you don't have twenty-five minutes to relax. It's a quick fix to get you into the right mind space so you drink from a much calmer and logical space.

The **Hypno Blast 2** is for your social drinking. Listen to it before you go drinking socially. It is important you find somewhere warm and safe where you won't be disturbed. During this five-minute recording there are key messages to support sober social communication. It's about getting your mind into the right headspace to build natural self-esteem too.

ACKNOWLEDGEMENTS

I want to thank my eternally patient partner Ian, who has supported me so much with all the risks that come with being self-employed! You have been such an inspiration when the ideas were dry and my energy has been low. I love you infinitely!

Thank you to our beautiful triplet boys Ollie, Finn and Hugh for your cuddles, giggles and love. You inspire me every day to be in the moment.

Infinite thanks to my amazing parents Beverley Anne and Richard. You gave me the wings to be free to choose my life path without judgement. You gave me courage when I needed it, to do things out of my comfort zone.

Thank you to my beautiful sister, Ghinni. You have been an amazing support personally and professionally and you are the best Aussie aunty!

A big hug thanks to Val and Tom Mason, the best parents-in-law a girl could ever ask for.

A massive abundantly full of gratitude hug to all my clients, seminar participants and online purchasers. You have helped me to grow professionally every day. You have taught me so much more than you could ever imagine.

ABOUT THE AUTHOR

Georgia Foster qualified with distinction at the London College of Clinical Hypnosis and has been working as a clinical hypnotherapist since 1995. She has been featured in some of the most well read newspapers and magazines such as *The Sunday Times*, the *Guardian*, *Metro*, *Good Housekeeping*, *Psychologies* and *Cosmopolitan*. She is a regular guest on Sky News and The Morning Show (Australia).

Georgia's self help on-line programs sell everyday around the world.

- The 3 Minute Anxiety Fix, anxiety reduction
- The Weight Less Mind, stop emotional overeating
- Believing In You, improve self esteem
- Thinking Fertile, supporting emotional confidence to conceive
- Cracking The Love Code, helping women to change their thinking about love
- The Fearless Speaker, improve public speaking confidence
- The Fearless Musician, improve musical performance
- Mastering Your Twenties Blueprint, helping people in their 20's build self esteem

After living in London since 1994, Georgia moved back to Australia in 2017 with her partner Ian and their triplet boys, Ollie, Finn and Hugh.

Georgia's 1 day Drink Less Mind seminar runs regularly in the UK and Australia.

Please see more www.georgiafoster.com